SPORTS SCIENCE

THE SCIENCE OF SOCCER

AMY B. ROGERS

ROSEN PUBLISHING

Published in 2026 by The Rosen Publishing Group, Inc.
2544 Clinton Street, Buffalo, NY 14224

Portions of this work were originally authored by Jenny MacKay and published as *Soccer*. All new material this edition authored by Amy B. Rogers.

Designer: Rachel Rising
Editor: Jill Keppeler

Cataloging-in-Publication Data

Names: Rogers, Amy B.
Title: The science of soccer / Amy B. Rogers.
Description: Buffalo, NY : Rosen Publishing, 2026. | Series: Sports science | Includes glossary and index.
Identifiers: ISBN 9781499479515 (pbk.) | ISBN 9781499479522 (library bound) | ISBN 9781499479539 (ebook)
Subjects: LCSH: Soccer--Juvenile literature. | Sports sciences--Juvenile literature.
Classification: LCC GV943.25 R64 2026 | DDC 796.334--dc23

Manufactured in the United States of America

CPSIA Compliance Information: Batch #CSRYA26. For further information, contact Rosen Publishing at 1-800-237-9932.

CONTENTS

FOREWORD

The way that high-caliber athletes perform can seem unbelievable. To many people watching in the stands or from home, their feats may seem unreal—as unlikely as learning to fly. Even regular players and participants in these sports may stare in awe, feeling like they can never reach those heights.

However, the laws of nature are still the law and still unbreakable, and once you learn more about how the science behind these sports works, they're in some ways even more amazing. Peak athletes use the laws of nature and science to achieve their unbelievable feats, and understanding these laws can give you an even greater appreciation for their achievements. Science makes the incredible understandable and the seemingly unreal real. Rather than ruining an appreciation for sports, it can deepen our understanding and increase our awe.

In these books, readers can learn more about the scientific ideas behind athletic achievements, from the simplest hit in baseball to the most amazing gymnastics flip. Physics principles such as gravity, friction and drag, and Newton's laws of motion can all be applied to sports—and this means all sports, including swimming, football, track, and lacrosse. Readers will also learn about other scientific aspects of sports, including the whys and hows of athletic training, the principles of sports medicine, and the advances in technology that will affect these fields for years to come. This understanding can help young athletes better train for their sport, avoid injury, and better care for injuries when they happen.

These principles and ideas are presented in clear, understandable ways, with relatable and clear examples, including quotes from those who play and participate in the sports, those who coach and help them, and those who study the science behind it all.

Sports and science are intrinsically intertwined. The basic principles of sports are the basic laws of science, and understanding one side will help you understand the other better. This is true for sports fans and young scientists alike!

Understanding the science behind sports allows us to better appreciate what athletes can do.

CHAPTER ONE

THE MOST POPULAR SPORT

Soccer in the United States is in something of an odd position. It's not even called by the name that's used in much of the world. In many (but not all) other countries, the sport is called football, association football, or a variation on that name, while in the United States and Canada, that word means a different game entirely, one that tends to be far more popular in the United States than association football.

That said, overall, soccer is the world's most popular sport. This is partly because it can be played very easily, with fewer resources than many other sports. While it can be (and often is) played in major stadiums around the world, it can also be played on any bit of land available, whether it's an open field or an empty lot. Players just need a ball and something to serve as a goal.

In one form or another, soccer has been around for thousands of years. Joseph "Sepp" Blatter, a former president of the Fédération Internationale de Football Association (FIFA)—the international governing body of professional soccer—once said, "Football is as old as the world … People have always played some form of football, from its very basic form of kicking a ball around to the game it is today."[1] Although soccer might not be quite as old as Earth itself, it does have roots in games played by ancient civilizations.

Although ancient athletes may not have thought about it at the time, they put science into action every time they kicked a ball and ran across a playing field, or pitch. Today's soccer players and those who work with them have a better

FREE KICKS As of 2025, about 240 million people around the world play soccer. A relatively small percentage of them are in the United States.

understanding of how science factors into their performance on the pitch, and coaches, players, and scientists have used that knowledge to come up with better equipment, more efficient training programs, and more effective injury treatment.

KICKING IT IN ANCIENT TIMES

Kicking games arose from more than one culture across history. It is tough to know when and where they first started. Some of the earliest records of a kicking game that resembled soccer come from China. About 200 BCE, the Chinese invented a kickball-style sport that used a round ball made of leather and stuffed with silk, fur, hair, or feathers. Players were divided into two teams, and the game was played on an area with marked edges to define the boundaries. There was a goal— a net pulled taut between two bamboo poles—in the middle of the playing area. The net had a hole about 12 inches (30 cm) wide for the ball to pass through so a team could score. Like the modern sport of soccer, players in this early Chinese ball game were able to use any body part except their hands. The sport was called *cuju* or *tsu' chu*.

Several centuries after the first records of cuju, the Japanese created their own ball-kicking game called *kemari*, which used a deerskin ball that was 9 to 10 inches (23 to 25 cm) in diameter and stuffed with sawdust. Players set out to keep the ball from touching the ground by juggling it—keeping it in the air and passing it to other players using their feet, knees, and chests but not their hands. Kemari games consisted of eight men, and they played within the boundaries of a field marked by specific trees in each corner—cherry, maple, willow, and pine. The sport did not pit one team against another; rather, everyone on the field worked together with the common objective of keeping the ball from touching the ground. Once a certain number of consecutive "juggles" had

Shown here is a modern example of kemari in Japan.

been accomplished, which could be up to 1,000, the game was over.

Ball-kicking games in ancient China and Japan were more than just ways for people to kill time. The games also served important purposes in society. Kemari was sometimes played as part of Japanese religious ceremonies. Cuju was sometimes used as a form of military training and also was linked to traditional Chinese ideas and ways of thought.

According to historian Nigel B. Crowther, "Ancient handbooks (including one of the earliest surviving Chinese texts) show how important cuju grew to be in Chinese society."[2] He has said the game was even seen to represent traditional, spiritual Chinese ideas, such as the opposite concepts of yin and yang. Games such as cuju were very symbolic in ancient cultures because they represented the world as the people understood it at the time. The field was a symbol of the earth, for example, and the ball symbolized a heavenly body such as the sun. There may also have been kicking games played in other parts of Asia around this time.

MAJOR LEAGUE SOCCER

While soccer is not as huge in North America as it is in other countries around the world, its popularity has been growing. Major League Soccer (MLS) is North America's main professional soccer league. As of 2025, there are 27 MLS teams in the United States and three in Canada. The league was founded in 1993 and started play in 1996. It was preceded by the North American Soccer League from 1968 to 1984.

The first few years of the league were marked by financial losses, but matters eventually turned around as soccer's popularity in North America grew. The season starts in February or March and runs until October, followed by the MLS Cup playoffs. The 2024 MLS champion was the LA Galaxy, which has the most championships of any team in the league.

The newest MLS team as of 2025 is San Diego FC. The three Canadian teams are based in Toronto, Vancouver, and Montreal.

IN THE AMERICAS

Other cultures and areas also developed their own kicking games. These games also reflected their culture's religious and philosophical beliefs. Some of the people of ancient North, South, and Central America had an especially strong spiritual connection to kicking games, which may have older origins than the games played by ancient cultures in Asia. The long history of ball games in the Americas has been demonstrated in Paso de la Amada in Mexico, where modern archaeological digs have turned up a field believed to have been used to play ball games that is estimated to be 3,500 years old. Some historians believe ball-kicking sports were played by every society in Central America. Soccer historian and author David Goldblatt has said, "The sheer number of courts and ubiquity of objects indicated that the game was played informally by commoners as well as ritually by the elite."[3]

The ancient Maya, who lived in the rain forests of Mexico and Central America, placed extreme importance on kicking games, so much so that their beliefs about the very creation of their culture were rooted in a ball game in which two twin brothers defeated the gods and later became the sun and moon in the sky. It was not uncommon for players of Maya ball games to be sacrificed to the gods at the end of a match.

Ball games were so important to the Maya that their playing fields had phenomenal proportions. One of the world's most famous ancient landmarks is the Great Ball Court at the Maya ruins of Chichén Itzá, an archaeological site on modern-day Mexico's Yucatán Peninsula. The ball court is almost twice the size of a modern soccer field. It has a temple-like structure at either end, perhaps where ancient royalty gathered to watch important games. Despite the field's enormous size and the fact that it is open to the sky, a human whispering at one end of the court could be heard clearly by someone standing at the other end. The acoustics (physical properties that determine how sound travels) of the Great Ball Court remain a mystery, but the parallel walls along the length of the field are believed to create a "flutter echo" effect in which sound waves bounce from wall to wall to carry sounds up or down the court.

Shown here is the Great Ball Court of the Maya.

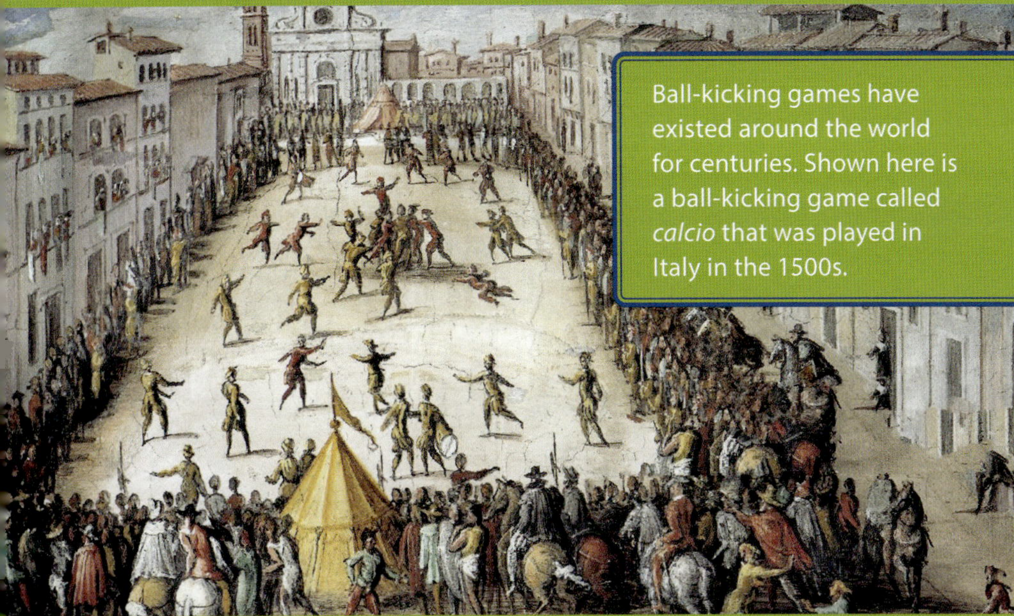

Ball-kicking games have existed around the world for centuries. Shown here is a ball-kicking game called *calcio* that was played in Italy in the 1500s.

The attention paid to every small detail of the Great Ball Court, even its acoustics, shows the importance that ball-kicking games had in Maya culture and, historians believe, in nearly every other culture of Central America leading up to European colonization in the 1400s and 1500s. "In some Latin American areas soccer is simply called *pelota* (ball)—as if the only ball game existing or imaginable is soccer," author Richard Witzig wrote. "This illustrates the central cultural position soccer occupies in Latin American countries."[4]

Ball-kicking games were also played in other parts of the Americas. When the first English colonists arrived on the North American coast in what is now the state of Massachusetts in 1620, they wrote about Native Americans playing a ball game called *pasuckquakkohwog*, or "they gather to play ball with the foot." And when the Spanish colonized Central America and South America, they discovered something even more unique about American ball games—many American balls bounced because they were made from the sap of rubber trees native to this part of the world. Ball games played with rubber balls were far different from those played with the heavy, feather-stuffed, leather balls used elsewhere in the world.

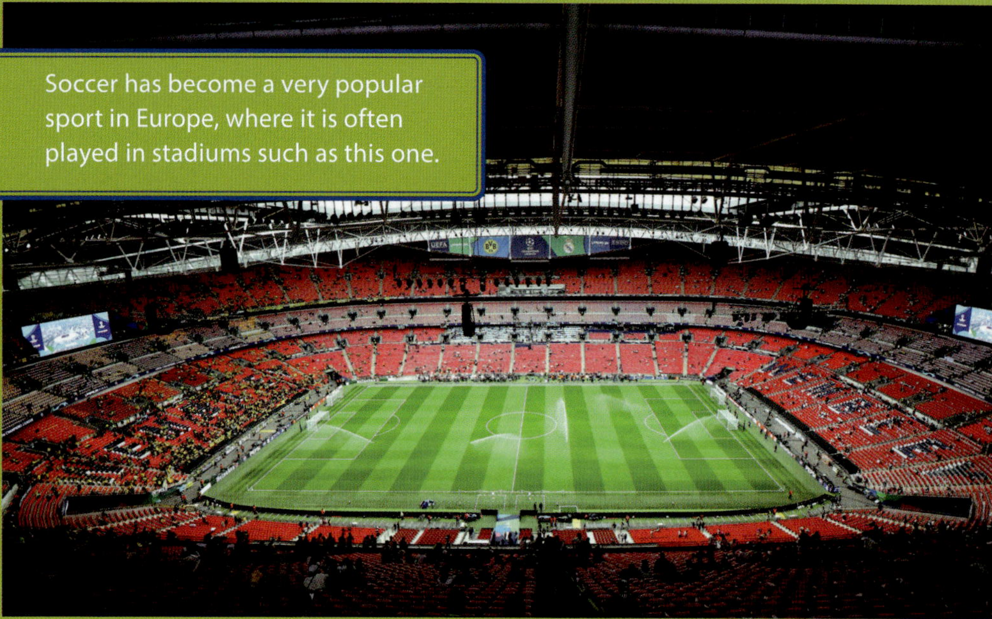

Soccer has become a very popular sport in Europe, where it is often played in stadiums such as this one.

SOCCER IN EUROPE

The ancient Greeks and Romans also played various forms of ball games. These included the ancient Greek game of *episkyros* and the ancient Roman game of *harpastum*. In episkyros, teams of young Greek men battled on a field to throw and kick a ball over a central line while trying to force the opposing team over its rear boundary line, which was the key to winning the game. Harpastum was similar to the modern-day children's game of keep-away or pickle-in-the-middle. The object was to throw and kick the ball away from someone else. Games similar to episkyros and harpastum were still played around Europe in the 19th century.

The games that eventually inspired the development of soccer were especially popular in England. In English society, sports had always been sharply divided along class lines between rich and poor. Favorite sports of the wealthy, such as hunting and polo played on horseback, differed from the favorite sports of the lower classes, such as ball-kicking games that required nothing but a ball and two teams willing to play. By the 1700s and 1800s, ball games—also known as "folk football"—among

FREE KICKS The word "soccer" was first used by the British as an abbreviation of "association football," or football played without using the hands, as opposed to "rugger," or rugby-style football, which allows players to use their hands.

the lower classes had evolved into wildly popular and often violent matches. Entire neighboring towns sometimes battled against one another in the struggle to move the ball across the other team's goal. English ball games were officially banned by various kings at different times in history, because they were believed to threaten public safety and social order.

Then, a new tradition came about in English society—boys' schools, where upper-class young men went to live and to learn. The boys who attended these schools had few ways to spend free time because they were away from home, so they took up ball games. Schools formed teams and competed against other schools. These teams quickly learned that they could not play fairly against each other without a standard set of rules, so they created ball game regulations. The groundwork of modern-day soccer as an international, organized sport was laid in the mid-1800s in the schools of England, such as Eton. It is still popular in such settings today.

DIFFERENT RULES

These earlier soccer games in England also used different rules or rules that varied by school. Some allowed hands to be used during play, while at other schools, the use of hands was forbidden. As the schoolboys grew up, they took their favorite versions of soccer with them to the universities they attended. The debate over whether hands should be used in college ball games became heated, with different schools taking different sides. The first notable attempt to standardize the rules of soccer occurred in 1846 with the establishment of the "Cambridge rules," which came from the University of Cambridge. Then, in 1863, the first official organization for the sport, the Football Association (FA), was formed in London. The members of this association wrote a set of official national rules to govern the sport.

The most controversial rule was the no-hands rule, forbidding the use of hands to touch the ball or to hold or grab other players during a game. Players who preferred the hands-on version of soccer started their own sport, rugby. Although rugby is also a popular sport, it was soccer that secured the top place in the hearts of the people of England, then Europe, then the world. Soccer became a worldwide phenomenon during the decades following that first official set of rules in 1863. These rules remain much the same in soccer today.

THE SPORT SPREADS

The "new" version of soccer immediately started to spread. Born during the Industrial Revolution, a period of new technology, new ideas, and new ways of living, the sport of soccer was positioned to enjoy a kind of success the human race had never before experienced in a pastime. Newspapers and telegrams became efficient ways to inform people about official rules of the new sport and to report on the outcomes of games. People in many different areas began to read about new teams and official matches in newspapers. The Industrial Revolution also brought new transportation to Europe in the form of trains, which made it possible for soccer teams to travel longer distances for games. This became increasingly important as England's fellow European countries put together their own soccer teams. Whenever there was a game to watch, local spectators flocked to the soccer field. Entire towns and cities rallied around their team on game day and squeezed in for a space in another new phenomenon—the sports stadium, built to house soccer matches and the fans who turned out in droves to watch.

Seeing an opportunity for profit, organizers of soccer teams began charging admission for spectators to see a game. The Industrial Revolution was an era of paid factory and office jobs, and many workers in England and across Europe spent money they made at their factory jobs watching soccer games. So powerful was the love of this new sport that it even changed the length of the average workweek. Since most soccer matches took place on Saturday, it became customary for employers to

A SOCCER LEGEND

Edson Arantes do Nascimento was born in 1940 in Brazil. He was nicknamed Pelé when he was young, and he played soccer in the dirt streets of his Brazilian hometown before becoming the sport's most famous star. Pelé played his first game for Brazil's national team when he was 16 years old, and he played in his first World Cup in 1958 at age 17. Pelé was part of teams that led Brazil to three World Cup titles (1958, 1962, and 1970).

During Pelé's 22-year career, he scored a total of 1,281 goals. He excelled at every aspect of the game, and his incredible play helped the sport of soccer grow and find new fans.

Named the FIFA Player of the Century (an honor shared with Argentina's Diego Maradona), Pelé was a sports legend the world over. He will forever be known as someone who helped his sport reach new heights of popularity because of his unique skills. He died in 2022 but is still remembered as one of the greatest to play the game.

give their workers Saturday afternoon off in order to watch games. Before that, Saturday had been a full workday.

As soccer brought about changes to European society, the feverish love of the sport traveled across continents and oceans to reach nearly every corner of the world. Central American and South American cultures took naturally to the sport, which was not dissimilar from games they had been playing for thousands of years. Soccer is still not as popular in the United States, though, as it is in other nations around the world. However, a growing number of young Americans are participating in and watching soccer. As of 2025, about 3 million kids in the United States play the sport.

MODERN SOCCER

While it may not be at the top in the United States, soccer is still the most-played and the most-watched sport on the planet. More than 200 of the world's nations and territories belong to FIFA. More than 1 billion people watch one or more soccer games during a World Cup tournament, which is the most

THE U.S. WOMEN'S SOCCER TEAM

In the United States, women's soccer did not really take off until the 1970s, with the passage of legislation called Title IX that allowed for equal athletic opportunities for male and female students in federally funded schools. Girls and women began playing soccer in schools, and the sport then began to grow in popularity.

The U.S. Women's National Team (USWNT) has become a dominant force on the world soccer stage. The team won the World Cup in 1991, 1999, 2015, and 2019. It also won Olympic gold medals in 1996, 2004, 2008, 2012, and 2024. Many of the most famous and successful soccer stars of the past and present in the United States are women, including Mia Hamm, Carli Lloyd, Megan Rapinoe, and Abby Wambach, who, as of 2025, is second in most goals scored in international competition by any soccer player.

Shown here is the USWNT after winning the gold medal at the 2024 Olympics.

famous international tournament in soccer. An average of 571 million viewers watched the whole World Cup Final (between Argentina and France) live in 2022, with more than 1.4 billion people watching at least one minute of the game.

"It's the moment when the planet becomes a family, when we're all doing the same thing whether we are in California or Nigeria or Shanghai,"[5] writer Simon Kuper said when describing the World Cup Finals.

One explanation for soccer's overwhelming worldwide popularity is that the sport is accessible to everyone. Almost anyone can learn to play soccer, no matter what gender they are or whether they are large or small, muscular or graceful, old or young. This is likely an important reason why the game is popular around the world, in wealthy countries as well as in developing ones. Soccer stars can come from anywhere and from any walk of life, and soccer has had a universal appeal since its earliest days. It is, as Witzig said, "almost as if the human collective consciousness willed the game of soccer into being."[6]

It is all a lot more deliberate than that, however. Soccer is a combination of various scientific factors at work, including the forces needed to kick the ball into the goal, the energy required to run across the pitch, and the body systems that must work together to allow players to perform at their best. Long before people understood the science behind soccer, those factors were still there and part of the game. As the sport has grown and changed, so has some fans' and players' understanding of the role of science in every moment of a soccer match. This can heighten enjoyment of all aspects of the world's most popular sport.

CHAPTER TWO

PHYSICS LESSONS

Many types of science are involved in soccer. However, physics may be the most involved. Physics is the science of matter and energy and how they interact. There is a lot of matter and energy on display in a soccer game! Kicking the ball to another player or toward the goal might not seem like a big deal, but many physics concepts are demonstrated in that one action. Physics in soccer deals with the physical properties of the ball, the energy used to kick it, the forces that keep it moving toward its target, and the way the field itself works to speed up or slow down the movement.

To those watching, soccer might not always seem like the most exciting game. Bursts of great action might not seem as frequent as in some other sports. However, if you understand the physics behind soccer, you will be better able to appreciate the sport, its players, and every move on the pitch.

PITCH PERFECT

People throughout the world play soccer, so it is important that there is a standard set of rules for everyone. One thing official rules specify is the size of the rectangular soccer pitch. The perimeter, or the outer edge of the field, is marked with white lines. There is a goal box at the center point of each short end of the field, with a penalty area marked in front of the goal box. A centerline is also marked across the exact middle of the field. Many soccer rules, such as whether the ball can remain in play or has gone out of bounds and where players can stand during a penalty kick, depend on these lines. A typical

Soccer fields used for official games must have the correct dimensions.

soccer field for adult players is about 74 yards (67.7 m) wide by 105.2 yards (110 m) long, which is slightly larger than the size of an American football field.

In an official soccer match, two teams of 11 players face off. One player on each team is the goalkeeper, who attempts to keep the ball out of the goal, preventing the other team from scoring. The goalkeeper, or goalie, can use their hands. With a total of 22 players moving on the field at one time, the field's dimensions are extremely important. "There must be a general relation between the number of players and the best size of the pitch," author John Wesson said. He continued:

> *The essential factor is that there be pressure on the players to quickly control the ball and decide what to do with it. This means that opposing players must typically be able to run to the player with the ball in a time comparable with the time taken to receive, control, and move the ball. If the distance between players is larger, the game loses tension. If the distance is much less the game has the appearance of a pinball machine.*[7]

The size of an official soccer field and the number of players per team were not chosen at random. A field's dimensions are meant to give both teams a fair chance at stealing the ball from each other and at passing it effectively among their teammates. The field's size helps determine how players position themselves within it. They must gauge how fast the ball can travel, for example, and what trajectory the ball will take—whether it will rise over the heads of players or drop quickly to the ground. These details, governed by physics, determine whether and how fast a soccer ball will reach its intended recipient during a pass without rolling out of bounds. Good players will pay attention.

LAWS OF MOTION

Soccer has rules that govern its play and its pitch. Other natural rules and law also affect it, of course. Resting objects, such as soccer balls, stay still if no force acts on them, and whenever a certain amount of force is applied to a resting object, it moves with predictable force. These phenomena were first described in the late 1600s by an English physicist named Isaac Newton, who described the behavior of any moving object with three simple statements, now known as Newton's laws of motion.

Newton's first law of motion states that a moving object will stay in motion at the same speed, in a straight line, until another force acts on it to change its velocity, or the rate at which it changes position. His second law states that there is a relationship between the mass of an object and the amount of force that must be applied in order to move it at a specific velocity. The third law of motion states that for every action, such as kicking a soccer ball, there is an equal and opposite reaction.

Newton's three laws are some of the most important facts in physics—and soccer games. Knowing that the velocity at which a resting object will move depends on the force applied to it, soccer players plan the force of their kicks to control the ball, keep it away from the other team, and move toward the other team's goal. They use knowledge of physics—what the ball will do once it is in motion—to position themselves close enough to or far enough from their team-

The laws of motion can be applied to everything you see on a soccer field, from the ball to the players themselves!

mates and opponents to have the best chance of completing, receiving, and intercepting passes. They also understand that any action, such as intercepting a ball, will cause an opposite reaction—a ball that hits a solid surface will naturally bounce the other way.

According to Newton's first law of motion, a resting soccer ball will not move until someone kicks it, and the direction and strength of the kick are essential. If a kick is too hard, the ball will sail over the players' heads and out of bounds. If a kick is too soft, it will move slowly, giving the other team an opportunity to dash in and steal it. Skilled soccer players have learned to kick with just the right amount of force. They must use their

FREE KICKS Newton's first law of motion is sometimes called the law of inertia because inertia is the resistance an object has to a change in its motion.

ON THE MOVE

Soccer players are often in motion around the pitch—running toward the goal, running to break up a pass, or moving to stop a shot. However, not all motion in a soccer game is the same, so it needs to be measured differently.

Speed measures the rate at which something moves. The direction an object moves does not matter when measuring speed. For example, soccer players can show speed when they run, even if they end up back where they started on the field. On the other hand, velocity measures the rate at which something changes its position, so the direction of movement matters. To show velocity, an object needs to move away from where it started. A soccer player can show this by running down the field to score a goal.

Acceleration is another way motion is measured. It is the measurement of how much an object's velocity changes over time. When velocity increases, the object is said to be accelerating. A soccer player accelerates when they increase their velocity to move faster than the defenders around them to reach the goal.

muscles to harness a certain amount of energy. This energy is then passed to a soccer ball during a kick. This sets it in motion.

GRAVITY: IT'S THE LAW

Another factor at play during a soccer game is gravity, or the pull of Earth on other objects. Soccer players adapt their kicks and their awareness of where the ball is and where it is going to accommodate for this force. The more mass an object contains, the stronger its gravitational pull. Because Earth contains much more mass than any person or object on it, the planet exerts a force of gravity that pulls things on its surface down toward it.

The force of gravity counteracts an object's tendency to stay in motion in a straight line. When a soccer ball sails into the air, there is a point at which it can rise no higher; the pull of Earth's gravity overcomes the ball's upward motion and starts bringing it back down to the ground. Gravity is what makes a ball move in an arc after a hard kick—it rises, and then it begins to come back down to Earth. Experienced soccer players can predict when and where the ball will descend, positioning themselves near the point where it will come back down so they can try to intercept it.

A soccer ball's trajectory can also be affected by environmental forces, such as wind. If the wind and the ball are moving in opposite directions, then the blowing wind will create a force of resistance against the ball. In short, the ball will not go as far unless a player kicks harder to compensate for the force of the wind. Even balls kicked along the ground are subject to resistance in the form of friction, which is a force created whenever two surfaces rub or slide against each other. Soccer balls experience friction when they roll or bounce along the ground, especially on surfaces such as the grass of the playing

Friction exists between a soccer ball and the ground and between a soccer player's cleats and the ground.

field. Long grass, which has more surface area, will create more friction, absorb more of the ball's energy, and slow the ball down faster than short grass will.

A soccer player is constantly considering basic facts of physics, such as the laws of motion, gravity's pull on the ball, wind resistance, and friction, throughout a game. "Does the player use physics formulas? Of course not," engineers Seyed Hamid Hamraz and Seyed Shams Feyzabadi have said. However, they added, "We can firmly express that the player [learns] by way of experience."[8] Practice gives a soccer player an innate understanding of physics principles as related to the game.

SCORING A GOAL

A soccer ball controlled by players must overcome gravity, friction, and the actions of other players to make it into the goal. Like the size of the soccer field, the size of the goal boxes is important to the outcome of a soccer match. A standard goal in an adult soccer game is a metal frame 24 feet (7.3 m) wide by 8 feet (2.4 m) tall. These dimensions give the goalkeeper a fair chance at defending the entire goal and the opposing team a fair chance at getting the ball past the goalkeeper and scoring.

The best goalkeepers and goal scorers in the world are fairly evenly matched. "A top-class goalkeeper can cover the whole of the goal given a little more than a second," Wesson explained, and a good kicker "can kick the ball at 80 miles [129 km] per hour."[9] This is why the dimensions of the goal were carefully chosen to ensure that neither the player trying to score nor the player trying to stop them had too much of an advantage. A larger goal would be too difficult for a goalkeeper to defend, making goals too easy to score. A smaller goal would make it almost impossible for the opposing team to score. Specific dimensions for the goal box help make a soccer game fair for both teams. Practice gives players a feel for those dimensions so that, when they are out on the pitch, they can judge what combination of forces is needed to score a goal.

BENDING IT LIKE BECKHAM

David Beckham is a famous soccer player known for his skill at "bending" a soccer ball's trajectory around players to score. This skill actually has a scientific name: the Magnus effect. The Magnus effect is caused by changes in velocity as an object moves through a liquid or gas, such as air. In soccer, the Magnus effect can be seen when a spinning soccer ball moves through the air. The resistance, or drag, caused by the air around the ball slows the movement of the air on one side of the ball and speeds up the air's movement on the opposite side. This causes a difference in air pressure, and the ball's trajectory bends toward the lower air pressure on the side where the air is moving faster. The way a soccer ball's path curves when the Magnus effect is at work is commonly called a "banana kick" because the trajectory is curved like a banana.

The Magnus effect is seen in many other sports, too. If a ball is spinning through the air, you'll be able to see the Magnus effect in action. In baseball, the Magnus effect is the reason curveball pitches curve. Golfers use the Magnus effect to bend their shots around things that are in their way, such as trees.

Soccer superstar David Beckham is shown here.

ON THE FIELD

There are standard measurements and dimensions to a soccer field for very good reasons. However, there is more to a balanced soccer field than this. To make sure a match is fair, fields must be literally balanced, meaning that they do not slope from one end to the other. They also cannot have hills, dips, or craters. An uneven field can make the game more difficult for one team than the other. It can also lead to an added risk of injuries for the players.

People who design competitive sports fields use physics to create level playing surfaces that are safe and fair for both teams.

An uneven playing surface can create unfair playing conditions.

FREE KICKS As of 2025, Brazil has the most men's FIFA World Cup titles at five, won in 1958, 1962, 1970, 1994, and 2002.

First, the area must be mostly flat. A field cannot slope noticeably from side to side, because a slope will affect the movement of the soccer ball. A ball that lands on a flat surface will stay put, but a ball that lands on a slope will begin to roll down the slope due to the force of gravity, and this will affect everything about how the soccer game is played. The ball may go out of bounds more often, for example, if the field is sloped in a way that makes it roll outside the perimeter line of the field. Every time a ball goes out of bounds, play must stop while a player throws the ball back in. This interrupts the flow of the game and is frustrating for players and spectators.

Even worse than a field that slopes from side to side is one that slopes from end to end. The team whose goal is on the downhill end of the slope will be at a distinct disadvantage. The players will constantly be fighting the ball's tendency to roll toward their own goal. They will also have to run uphill against the slope as they try to move the ball toward the opposing team's goal. This requires more energy than running on a flat field.

The players on the opposing team, meanwhile, will be working downhill; the ball will naturally roll in their favor, and it will take less physical effort to run toward the other team's goal. Even a slight slope, invisible to the naked eye, can make a difference in the efforts of the two teams and in the outcome of a game. The people who design soccer fields carefully measure for any slope in the area where they want to build a field. When people are building the field, they can add or remove dirt to help correct the slope.

WATER HAZARD

Correcting gradual slopes on a soccer field is important, but it is just as important to remove any abrupt hills or dips. A soccer player running at full speed and concentrating on other

FREE KICKS A soccer player runs an average of 6.4 miles (10.3 km) each game.

players and the ball may not see an uneven patch of ground and might stumble or trip. Not only will this interrupt the momentum of the game, but a player could also be injured. Therefore, field designers take extra care to make sure that a soccer field is without any uneven areas, such as bumps or craters.

Perfectly flat fields, however, can also pose problems. The physical properties of water and its tendency to puddle can have an effect on the outcome of a soccer game too. Water that falls on a soccer field during a rainstorm or from sprinklers watering the grass will have nowhere to go. It will form puddles or sheets of water, and these make their own hazards during a soccer game. Water molecules have a tendency to stick to one another, which is why water molecules form water droplets and why water droplets group together to form puddles. Whenever a ball rolls through a puddle, water droplets stick to it, and this can create problems in a game. A wet ball that has absorbed a small amount of water is slicker and slightly heavier than a dry ball, and this could affect the players' handling of it.

Still another problem with wet fields is that if soccer players step into puddles or soggy areas, they might slip, lose their footing, or miss an important pass or kick. This is because the water acts as a lubricant, or a substance that reduces friction. The reduced friction between a player's feet and the turf can be dangerous. "Each time a soccer player kicks the ball, he or she is by definition standing on one foot in a posture that requires good footing," Jim Puhalla, Jeff Krans, and Mike Goatley wrote in their manual for designing sports fields. "So evenness of the surface becomes an increasingly important issue for the safety and performance of the athletes."[10]

To prevent water from collecting on soccer fields, architects design the fields to avoid water buildup. They most often do this by adding an almost unnoticeable hill, or crown, down the center of the field lengthwise. This makes the field slope very slightly

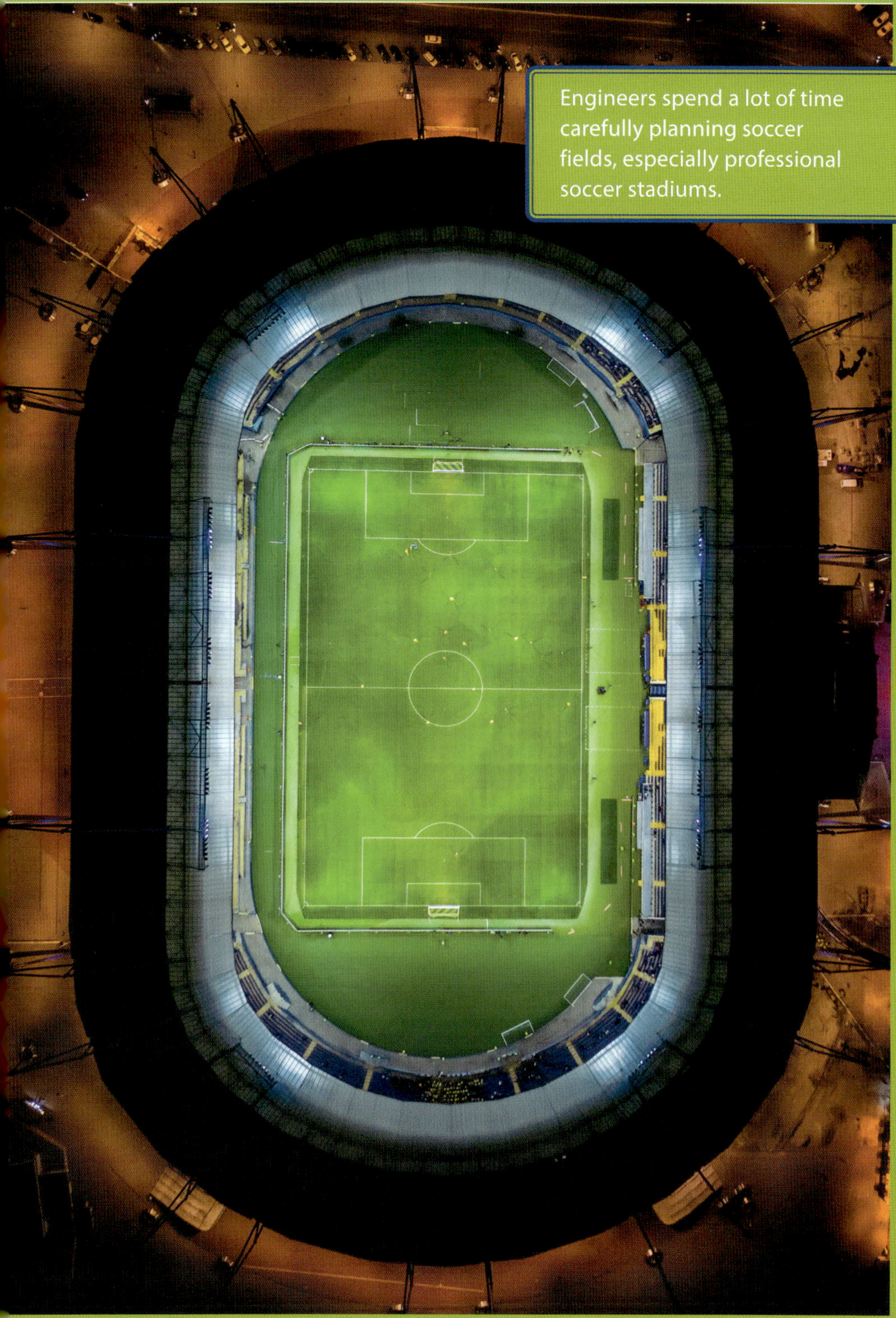

Engineers spend a lot of time carefully planning soccer fields, especially professional soccer stadiums.

THE RIGHT AMOUNT OF AIR

When a soccer ball is filled with air, it is actually being filled with many individual air molecules. Although air is invisible, it still has weight and takes up space. When many air molecules come together, they take up more space and begin to press against an object or surface. The force of this pressing is called air pressure. Air pressure is created in a container when air molecules get crammed together in one place. A soccer ball is a container because its bladder holds air. The air pressure inside the ball increases as more air is pumped into the ball.

A soccer ball must be filled with the right amount of air or it will not perform as expected. Air pressure affects an object's elasticity, or its ability to return to its normal shape after an outside force has attempted to change that shape. Lower air pressure means lower elasticity, so a soccer ball that is underinflated will not return to its original shape after being kicked. On the other hand, if a soccer ball is inflated with too much air, its bladder might break from the air pressure being too great for the container.

at a grade of about 1 to 2 percent from the center toward both sidelines. In other words, for every 12 inches (30 cm) of distance across the field from the center crown, the field will slope down about 0.25 inch (0.64 cm). With this slight slope, any water that collects on the field will trickle toward the sidelines instead of forming puddles on the playing surface. It is important that the slope is not enough to affect the rolling of the ball or the running of the players. The people who design soccer fields use their understanding of physics and math to make sure that the slope is just right to give players the best possible conditions.

ON THE BALL

Physics affects the way people design soccer playing fields. In addition, physics is critical to the key component of the game—the ball. A soccer ball is in nearly constant motion during a match as it is kicked, nudged, bumped off of heads, and caught by the goalkeeper. The ball's physical properties are designed specifically for the different ways it is put to use during a match.

The dimensions of soccer balls have changed little since the first official soccer rules were written in the late 1800s. Players realized that there is an optimal size and weight for a ball. Balls that are too heavy require too much strength to kick, and a heavy ball may cause head or neck injuries if a player uses her head to stop and redirect it. A ball that is too light, on the other hand, may not travel as players expect. It is much more vulnerable to wind resistance on a blustery day, for example. Bowling balls would be too heavy for use in a soccer game, and beach balls would not be heavy enough.

These examples demonstrate why mass (the amount of matter within an object of a certain size) and weight (the amount of gravitational pull Earth has on an object due to its mass) are important characteristics for a soccer ball. Even slight differences in size or weight can change the way a ball travels across the ground or through the air and could make a pass fall short of its target or a shot fly wide of the goal.

A standard soccer ball for adults is generally between 14 and 16 ounces (397 and 454 g), and its circumference—the distance around the circular shape—is generally between 27 and 28 inches (69 and 71 cm). These specifications are important because players expect a standard soccer ball to behave a certain way when kicked, dribbled, or bounced off the head. Similar to a field that has not been designed according to official regulations, a ball that has not been made according to official dimensions may change the flow or even the entire outcome of a game because it does not behave in a scientifically predictable way.

The shape of a soccer ball also needs to remain standardized to allow the game to play out in a safe, relatively predictable way. Because it is a ball, people often mistakenly say that it is a sphere. However, a soccer ball is actually a shape known as a truncated icosahedron. This is a shape with 60 vertices, or points. Soccer balls commonly have 12 pentagonal, or five-sided, faces and 20 hexagonal, or six-sided, faces. Each face is

Shown here is the soccer ball that was used during the 2022 FIFA World Cup. The latest technology and engineering went into the making of this ball.

stitched or glued on as its own patch, or panel. On a traditional soccer ball, the pentagonal faces are black, and the hexagonal faces are white. The faces are curved, so the ball has a shape close to a sphere without being perfectly spherical.

Although this design is the most common, it is not necessarily the best. Scientists and engineers are still working to determine the most aerodynamic shape for a soccer ball. Aerodynamics is the branch of science that deals with the way air moves around objects and the way objects move through the air. Soccer balls need to be aerodynamic in order to move easily through the air toward the goal or to another player. Scientists conduct tests and experiments to see how changes in a soccer ball's design affect its aerodynamics.

In part because of these tests, different soccer balls have been used at World Cup events in recent years. These balls were made from a decreasing number of panels. What started as 32 became 14 panels in 2006, 8 panels in 2010, and 6 panels in 2014. However, the Al Rihla ball used for the 2022 men's World Cup had 20 panels, as did the Al Hilm ball used in the semifinals and final.

ALL TOGETHER NOW

Many aspects of the game, including the dimensions of the field, the size of the goal boxes, and the design of the ball, come together to influence a soccer match. All these elements have scientific reasons behind their shape, size, and construction. Physics plays an important role in a soccer match, and soccer equipment and fields are designed with physics in mind.

The most important parts of a soccer game, of course, are the people playing it. The field, the goal, and the ball are there to be used by the players. They put the ball in motion using force and turn potential, or stored, energy into kinetic energy, or energy in motion. If you know the science behind it, every soccer game is a physics lesson in motion.

CHAPTER THREE

SCIENCE IN MOTION

The feats performed by the greatest soccer players on the pitch may seem impossible, or at least unlikely. One example came at the 2015 Women's World Cup, when American Carli Lloyd scored a hat trick—three goals—in just 16 minutes, helping her team beat Japan, 5–2, in the final. Hat tricks tend to be rare, and the timing and setting made the feat even more impressive. It made Lloyd look like a superhero, and indeed, her nickname is actually "Captain America."

Each of Lloyd's three goals was impressive, but perhaps the most incredible of them all was her third goal, which was a shot from the centerline that somehow made its way past the Japanese goalkeeper and into the net. As Nate Scott wrote in *USA Today*, "It didn't make any sense. It shouldn't have worked. But it worked."[11]

How did it work? A variety of scientific factors were at play, allowing Lloyd to send the ball flying through the air, behind the goalkeeper, and into the history books. Her ability to accelerate past defenders, keep her balance, and get just the right amount of force behind her kick can all be explained using biomechanics, or the science of movement.

The study of biomechanics aims to explain the body and its actions as the workings of a living machine. This is certainly true for superstar soccer players such as Lloyd, whose bodies are some of the most finely tuned machines in the world. A soccer player's body features many parts that work together to achieve athletic greatness. What might look simple to fans watching from their seat is often anything but simple when looked at

Carli Lloyd, shown here, retired in 2021, but her World Cup hat trick is still considered one of her sport's most impressive feats.

from a scientific perspective. Basic soccer skills such as running, kicking, and stopping the ball might seem basic, but they require body parts working in a certain way at the right time to accomplish them.

ART OF THE KICK

Soccer is called football in many countries for good reason. It is mostly a kicking game, a sport dominated by the work of the legs and feet. The foot is what comes in contact most often with the ball. However, in terms of mechanics, the foot is merely the end of the leg. With every kick of the ball, the foot functions like the snapping tip of a whip, but the whip itself—the entire leg—drives every kick.

FREE KICKS

The first FIFA Women's World Cup was played in 1991, 61 years after the first Men's World Cup was played.

In soccer, the human leg works as a system of levers—straight bars that rotate or pivot around a fixed point, or fulcrum, to apply force to another point (in this case, the ball). The straight bones of the leg—the femur in the thigh and the tibia and fibula that make up the shin—act as the bars of the lever. The fulcrums are the joints—the hip, knee, and ankle. Both portions of the leg—upper and lower—act as separate but related levers during a kick, combining their force and direction to make the foot connect with the ball with particular power or precision. Because the hip joint can rotate, it can move the upper leg not just backward and forward but diagonally and from side to side. The knee joint moves only forward and backward, but combined with the variety of angles possible at the hip, both joints work together to create a lever that can make contact with the ball from limitless directions and with various amounts of force. This force that is applied to the ball is fittingly known as applied force.

Controlling the direction and force of the leg and foot at the moment of a kick is the central skill of soccer. The velocity of the ball is related to the force used to move it—the strength of the kick. A good soccer player at the professional level has the ability to kick the ball an average of 98 feet (29 m) per second, but kicking that hard is not always an advantage. A ball that sails past its intended target—a teammate or the goal—does no good to anyone in a soccer game. Most soccer kicks, in fact, are designed to achieve a velocity that is well below what powerful kickers could achieve if they gave it their all. Often just a mere tap of the ball is needed, such as when players dribble, making short kicks to keep the ball in front of them as they run up the field. Soccer is not just a matter of pure power. It is also a matter of control and of judging the right amount of force to apply at the right moment to get the ball where the player needs it to go.

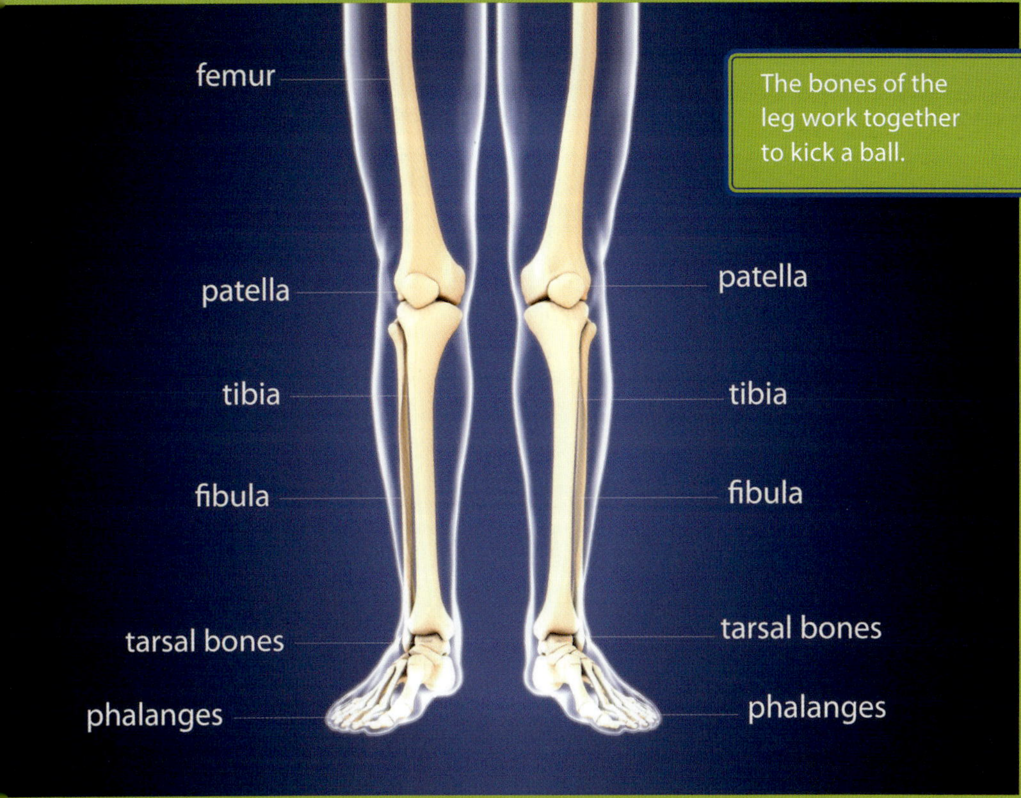

The bones of the leg work together to kick a ball.

MUSCLE POWER

The ability to apply just the right amount of force to the ball is controlled by muscles. (However, the choice to do it at exactly the right time is controlled by the brain.) Muscles are attached to and control the movement of bones, which in the case of kicking, means the direction and force of the lever system created by the legs. The quadriceps is the large muscle running down the front of the thigh. Along the back of the thigh are the hamstrings, and where the femur bone of the thigh connects to the hip are the hip flexor muscles. These are the major muscles responsible for moving the leg in a soccer kick.

The biomechanical action of a full-force kick happens in this way: First, the soccer player plants one foot on the ground as support. This frees up the opposite leg to work as the kicking

 There are 26 bones in each human foot.

HOW TO KICK

Soccer players do not typically kick the ball with the top of the foot or their toes. This way of kicking gives them too little control over the ball's direction. Instead, they kick with their instep, which is the inside of their foot. The instep has a greater surface area than the toe, which gives the player more control over where the ball is going.

Most soccer kicks also start from the side of the ball rather than from directly behind it. This is because approaching the ball from the side allows the soccer player's hip to rotate more than it could from a position directly behind the ball. Hip rotation allows for more force to be applied to the ball, which makes for a stronger kick.

lever. The player then extends the kicking leg as far back as necessary; the larger the swing of the lever, the more energy the foot can transfer to the ball and the more forceful the kick will be. Once the leg is extended backward, the hip flexor muscle at the front of the hip tenses to pull the thigh forward. When the knee is positioned over the ball, the hamstring muscle along the back of the thigh, which has been tensed to pull the lower leg backward, releases its tension. The powerful quadriceps, meanwhile, tenses to pull the lower leg and the foot forward. The shin swings down like a whip, and the foot, which is anchored by a stiff ankle so it works like the heavy end of a club, transfers the combined energy of the entire leg to its target, the ball.

The kick works like a chain reaction, gathering strength and momentum from the start of the backswing to the instant of impact, when the energy of the leg is transferred to the ball to set it in motion. Much of the game of soccer revolves around this basic bit of mechanics.

SETTING A TRAP

Kicking is very important in soccer. This also means that stopping the movement of a ball that has been kicked is just as important, because it allows players to intercept passes or keep the ball out of the goal. Stopping a moving soccer ball is called trapping, and it involves different biomechanical principles than kicking. The kick involves transferring energy to the ball to make it move, but the trap involves absorbing a moving ball's energy to slow it down.

Newton's first and second laws of motion state that a resting object stays still unless a force moves it, and whenever a certain amount of force is applied to an object, it will move predictably. Both are important concepts for soccer players, since they are the reason a soccer ball must be kicked with a certain amount of force in order for it to move the way players want. Newton's third law of motion is also very important in soccer. This law states that for every action, there is an equal and opposition reaction. Actions and reactions always occur in equal pairs. Whenever a moving soccer ball hits a solid surface, for example, the ball exerts a force on the surface at the moment of impact. The surface also exerts its own equal force back against the ball.

This concept of opposite reactions is critical in soccer, because when players are not dribbling or passing the ball, they are generally trying to trap it, placing themselves in front of it to stop its progress and make it fall to their feet so they can control it. Since no player other than the goalie can use their hands to catch the ball, stopping the ball's progress means placing some part of the body—the chest, the knee, the foot, the thigh, or even the head—directly in the path of the moving ball. However, Newton's third law of motion predicts that when a moving ball strikes another object, such as a human leg or torso, the ball will tend to bounce off and move the other way. To effectively trap a soccer ball and keep control of it, soccer players use special techniques to counteract Newton's third law of motion.

The trick to successfully trapping a moving ball is to absorb its energy. A soccer ball will not bounce off a flexible surface, such as a pillow, the same way it will bounce off a hard surface,

Practicing allows players to work on their trapping technique. Soccer practices are a great way to see science in action!

POTENTIAL AND KINETIC

There are two main kinds of energy, and both can be seen in a soccer match. Potential energy is the energy an object has because of its position. It is also known as stored energy. A soccer ball that has been trapped and is sitting at a player's feet has potential energy. The second kind of energy is kinetic energy, or energy of motion. An object has kinetic energy when it is moving. When a soccer ball is kicked after it has been trapped, it has kinetic energy.

The law of conservation of energy states that energy cannot be created or destroyed. It can only change forms. Therefore, when soccer players trap the ball, they are not removing energy, they are simply absorbing it. Kinetic energy becomes potential energy; it does not disappear. In the same way, when soccer players kick the ball, they are not creating new energy. The potential energy in the ball is being changed into kinetic energy by the force of the kick.

such as a brick wall. At the moment of impact, the flexible surface will move a little in the direction the ball is already going. The surface acts as a cushion, sinking in slightly to absorb some of the ball's force when the two objects collide. This will reduce the ball's tendency to bounce the opposite way. The wall, on the other hand, will not flex at the moment of collision. It will not cushion the impact or absorb the ball's energy, so the ball's movement in the opposite direction after the impact will be greater. To trap a ball, then, soccer players must try to cushion it—to absorb some of the moving ball's energy at the moment of impact. They do this by allowing their chest, thigh, knee, foot, or other body part to move a little in the same direction the ball is already going. This way, when the ball connects with a player's body, most of its energy is absorbed, not deflected. The ball will drop to the ground near the player's feet and remain in their possession instead of bouncing away toward opponents who could steal it. For this reason, this technique is very important for soccer players, just as important in some ways as kicking the ball.

Female soccer players tend to have a lower center of gravity than male soccer players, because women tend to have a lower center of gravity than men.

CENTER OF GRAVITY

Every object has a center of gravity, or single point at which the bulk of its weight is concentrated. The motion of any object can be described as the motion of its center of gravity from one place to another. Objects also turn or rotate around their center of gravity. So, to effectively trap a soccer ball by moving in the direction it is already going, the body's center of gravity is important. When soccer players attempt to trap a ball, they not only have to gauge the ball's center of gravity to understand its motion, they must also understand their own center of gravity—how and where they need to position themselves so they can absorb the force of the ball without being thrown off balance.

Center of gravity is closely tied to balance. Objects with a low center of gravity have their center point of weight positioned close to the ground—in general, these are broader, flatter objects that would be difficult to knock over. The higher the center of gravity, the easier it is for an object to topple. Young trees are a good example of how the center of gravity works. If a tree is tall and wispy, its center of gravity is higher off the ground. A strong wind will cause it to bend or even break. However, if the tree is short and solid, its center of gravity is low to the ground, and it is less likely to bend in the wind. Even if the two trees have the exact same weight and mass, the one with the lower center of gravity will be more difficult to knock over.

Soccer players use the same concept during a game, especially when they trap a ball. They may bend their knees slightly to lower their center of gravity so they can absorb the ball's impact with their body. If their center of gravity is too high, a forcefully kicked ball might knock them off balance when they try to trap it. Good soccer players have an innate understanding of their center of gravity and use it to their advantage on the field, helping them to move side to side to trap a ball or to change direction in an instant. "Athletes that need to be able to turn quickly know to keep their center of gravity low,"[12] civil engineer Cameron Bauer has stated. By keeping their center of gravity low, players are better able to change direction while maintaining their balance. This is a key part of the science of motion in soccer.

HEAD GAMES

Soccer players cannot use their hands during a game, so they also use their center of gravity to help make up for that. They fine-tune their ability to move their entire body toward a ball to stop or redirect its progress. One of the most unique skills in soccer is the use of the head to stop or move the ball. Like the act of kicking, where the weakest part of the leg—the foot—is

It is important for soccer players to learn proper heading technique to avoid serious injury.

what makes contact with the ball, the act of heading transfers force from a stronger part of the body—the trunk, made up of the back and chest—up through the neck to the striking point, which is the head. Often, the player jumps into the air to make contact with the ball, which means additional force is coming from the lower body, including the knees and hip flexors. The point of a header is not to have the ball hit the player in the head, but to have the player actively meet the ball in the air. The knees are bent and the torso is angled down when a player is in the proper position to execute a header. This keeps their center of gravity closer to the ground to maintain their balance and achieve maximum force to help redirect the force of the ball.

Using the head as a primary striking force seems as if it would cause serious injury, but heading is relatively safe because players train themselves to contract their neck muscles so that the neck and head themselves are not whipped forward but act as a stiff, clubbing surface. In addition, the use of the forehead helps remove some injury risk. This is a thicker part of the skull. It absorbs energy and force better and is less likely to be damaged.

ARMS AND HANDS

Soccer is not a game played without any use of the hands whatsoever. The rules state that hands and arms cannot be used by players other than the goalkeeper to catch the ball, change its direction, or push or grab other players. However, when soccer players are in action on the field, their hands and arms do not remain stiffly at their sides. Even though the arms of players besides the goalie do not actually touch the ball, they are used in almost every kick, header, and jump in the game. For one thing, arms held out to the sides help balance the body around its center of gravity, because having an equal amount of weight on both sides of the torso makes it more difficult for gravity to topple a person over. This is why it is easier for gymnasts to walk along a balance beam with their arms lifted away from the body and why arms held out to the sides act as a balancing mechanism when a soccer player is preparing to kick the ball.

The arms are used in soccer during headers too. They help players keep their balance, and when swung in a front-to-back motion, the arms add momentum and force to the forward motion of the torso during a header.

Whenever the ball rolls out of bounds in a soccer game, hands are important too. A game stops momentarily while a player throws the ball back into play, often by gripping the ball with both hands, bringing the arms back over the head, and flinging the ball back onto the field. A properly executed throw-in is often critical to a successful soccer game. "Restarts, or dead-ball situations, provide some of the best opportunities in soccer to create goal-scoring chances,"[13] soccer coach Gene Klein stated. At the same time, a botched toss from the sidelines can be intercepted by the opposing team, leading to a goal. "Players need to realize games can be won or lost in these situations,"[14] Klein added.

Understanding the biomechanics of arm movements can help players execute a successful throw-in. Like the

Soccer goalies, like wide receivers in American football, must have soft hands. This means they can catch a ball without it bouncing off their hands.

leg, the arm also acts as a lever, with the joints around it—the elbow, shoulder, and wrist—serving as fulcrums. The position of the arms and the amount of force they exert can help determine where the ball will land on a throw-in.

Nowhere on the soccer field are hands as important, however, as in the goal box. The goalkeeper is the one player on a soccer team allowed to use any part of the body that will help keep the ball out of the goal. (The goalkeeper may kick, trap, and even head a ball if that is the best way to stop the other team from scoring.) Goalkeepers are known for their ability to leap, dive, and tumble to catch the ball. They do this by instantaneously using principles of biomechanics and laws of motion. "Top goalkeepers have what we call *soft hands*," former soccer players Peter Mellor and Tony Waiters wrote. "They seem to be able to absorb the ball."[15] Goalkeepers do not technically absorb the ball, but they are able to keep it from bouncing off their hands by applying the principles of physics and biomechanics to their actions. They do not stiffen their hands completely; they allow for some flexibility when the ball touches them. This allows them to absorb some of the force of impact from the ball. Then, they are able to hold onto the ball instead of the ball bouncing off their hands—according to Newton's third law—and back into play. Practice helps them be able to do this with great control.

PRACTICE MAKES PERFECT

It may seem as though soccer players have a natural ability to make the most of biomechanical principles and physics on the pitch. To some degree, that may be true. However, most soccer players work very hard to achieve what looks like an effortless combination of skill and science. They train for long hours and condition their bodies to perform at their best. This training also requires a strong understanding of science to help athletes safely and successfully master the sport of soccer. Practice does not always make perfect, but it certainly can make an athlete's skills closer to it, so much that their abilities can seem superhuman to others.

CHAPTER FOUR

TRAINING SMART

All sorts of people play soccer. This includes people around the world and people of many different ages and body types. You do not have to be in peak physical shape to play and enjoy the game. Richard Witzig has stated, "There is no perfect soccer body."[16] However, pro or elite soccer players work hard to be in the best physical condition. Soccer—especially when played at its highest level—is a sport that demands a lot from the body. Soccer players need to develop the endurance required to run many miles during a game. They also need to develop the physical strength to power their kicks and sprint toward the ball or the goal, as well as the balance and coordination necessary to trap or head the ball.

Soccer players develop these physical abilities through long hours of training and conditioning. Their coaches often help them develop training programs that focus on specific body parts and skills. In some cases, soccer players have trainers who help them get their body in the best physical shape for peak performance on the pitch. Coaches, trainers, and players put careful thought into creating the right training programs and practice schedules. They take into account scientific principles, including biomechanical principles, and use their knowledge of the human body to ensure that each exercise has a specific purpose and is done safely.

Proper training is essential for professional soccer players and even for players on school or recreational teams. The right exercises help them develop their skills, strengthen their body, and prevent injury. Physical conditioning is one of the most important parts of game preparation. Another important part is fueling the body in the correct way. Learning about the science of nutrition helps soccer players know what foods to eat to give them long-lasting energy and help them build muscle in a healthy way.

Soccer played at a high level is not an easy sport. Former college soccer coach Ron McEachen has stated, "[Soccer players] do upwards of 200 sprints of varying distances, kick the ball 75 to 100 times, and jump to head the ball as many as 100 times. It's a physical game in which players make full-speed contact with each other as often as 50 times a game."[17] The proper training is important to ensure that players are physically prepared for the toll the sport can take on the body.

Soccer requires both physical fitness and technical skill. Players train hard to develop the coordination, muscle strength, endurance, and flexibility that will propel them through a physically challenging match. They also must train smart, using their scientific knowledge to understand both what can be done to improve their performance and the limits of the human body. This is important for training safely as well.

COORDINATION AND SOCCER

Hand-eye coordination is important in many sports, including soccer. The eyes constantly receive visual stimuli and send information to the brain about what they see. The brain, in turn, sends signals to the body through the central nervous system—the body's information gathering, processing, and control system—to respond to the visual stimuli. How accurately and quickly the hands reach for, grab, or manipulate an object once the eyes have seen it is a measure of hand-eye coordination. The ability to catch and throw a ball, for example, is second nature for most athletes, and the best can do it without ever looking at their hands—their brain intuitively measures the speed and the direction of an approaching ball and positions their hands perfectly for a catch. This is something soccer goalkeepers, for example, can do with amazing accuracy.

A slightly different skill is also needed in soccer: foot-eye coordination. It works much the same way as hand-eye coordination in that the feet have to respond quickly to what the eyes see. Foot-eye coordination is essential for basic tasks, such as running or climbing stairs—neither of which is easy to do with the eyes closed. The brain needs information from the eyes to direct the movement of the legs and feet. In soccer, foot-eye coordination is fundamental for kicking, dribbling, and trapping a ball. Pelé, who is widely considered one of the best soccer player of all time, said, "If you ever want to be a decent player, you have to learn to use each foot equally without stopping to think about it."[18]

Soccer training includes drills, such as dribbling through cones or kicking a ball repeatedly against a wall and intercepting it on the rebound, to develop the foot-eye coordination that the world's best soccer players have mastered. Although some level of foot-eye coordination is innate, it takes practice to develop the exceptional level of coordination the best soccer players

This dribbling drill is essential for developing strong foot-eye coordination.

display on a regular basis. These drills must be repeated over and over again to have an impact on the way the brain processes visual stimuli and the speed with which it sends messages to the feet. In time, it can become second nature.

THINKING FAST

The human brain coordinates body movements in response to visual stimuli. This allows soccer players to control the ball. It also guides their balance and reflexes. Balance is an essential soccer skill closely tied to foot-eye coordination. A soccer ball changes direction quickly as it gets passed from player to player. Running at full speed, soccer players keep their eyes on the ball and often must change direction in an instant without losing their balance. Balancing is a complicated process involving the vestibular system in the inner ear that contains fluid that shifts as the body moves. The ears send information back to the brain, which combines this information with what the eyes are seeing to signal the muscles to move in a way that restores balance and prevents falling down. Over time and with a lot of practice, soccer players' bodies get used to making abrupt turns in response to the movement of the ball without losing their balance at a critical moment in the game.

Another important factor in balancing is proprioception, or kinesthetic awareness. This is the body's sense of where it is in space. Even when soccer players cannot see all their limbs—for example, when focusing on the goal, they cannot constantly look at their feet—they have a sense of how their body is positioned because of proprioception. This "sixth sense" comes from sensors in the body's joints, muscles, and other tissues that send messages to the brain about the position and motion of body parts. These sensors are known as proprioceptors. A strong sense of proprioception is helpful for the development of good balance.

Coordination between the hands, feet, and eyes also relates to reflexes. A reflex is an involuntary, instantaneous response to a stimulus—something heard, seen, or felt. Blinking when an object flies toward your face is an example of a reflex. A person with slow reflexes may not even flinch or duck if an object were to fly at their face. A person with faster reflexes might have time to duck or put their hands up to deflect the object. An athlete with well-trained reflexes could catch the object. All soccer players must have good reflexes, but reflexes are especially important for goalkeepers. They must be able to respond instantaneously to the ball coming at the goal, putting their hands up to stop it before the other team scores.

It is possible to develop reflexes to respond more quickly to stimuli, especially visual ones. Improving coordination between the eyes, hands, and feet, for example, improves reflexes. Practicing any activity that requires coordination between the hands, feet, and eyes helps athletes develop better reflexes. Soccer drills to improve players' reflexes include having two players face off on the field. One prepares to kick the ball, and the other cannot move until the ball is in motion. The second player then must react quickly to intercept the moving ball. The closer the players stand to one another, the harder this drill will be and the better reflexes it will require. The more time spent practicing such activities, as well as playing actual soccer games, the better a player's reflexes will become. Most professional soccer players have practiced drills such as this one regularly for a long time.

BUILDING MUSCLES

Good coordination and reflexes are essential for soccer players. However, even before they start to master these important aspects of the game, soccer players must get their bodies in the right physical shape to handle playing in a soccer match. They need to be able to kick a soccer ball powerfully, for example. They also must be able to do things such as jog forward and backward, turn, leap to head the soccer ball, and break into a sprint throughout the full 90 minutes of a match without becoming exhausted or losing focus. To carry out these tasks, soccer players focus on two important aspects of fitness: strength and endurance.

Muscles give the body its strength and are the driving force behind any athletic performance. There are three types of muscle tissue: cardiac, smooth, and skeletal. Cardiac muscle tissue

PAIN AND PERSISTENCE

Few soccer players have demonstrated the physical toll the sport can have on the body as dramatically as former soccer superstar Michelle Akers. Her 15-year professional career began in 1985 with the USWNT's first international match and ended in 2000 due to a long list of physical ailments and injuries. Akers, who scored 105 goals in international matches and helped her team win two World Cup championship titles and an Olympic gold medal, is known as one of the best and toughest women to ever play the sport. On top of being battered with serious physical injuries that ranged from a dislocated shoulder to broken facial bones, Akers was also diagnosed with chronic fatigue syndrome, a long-term condition that results in extreme physical weakness and fatigue. The illness drained her body of the strength to sit up some days and caused severe migraine headaches and stomach problems. Still, Akers continued playing soccer for several years after her diagnosis, despite eventually requiring intravenous fluids after games. Akers left a legacy as one of the most dedicated players—of any gender—in the history of the sport.

is found in the heart, and smooth muscle tissue lines some of the other internal organs. These types of muscle tissue are not controlled voluntarily. The heart, for example, beats whether a person thinks about it or not. Skeletal muscle tissue, on the other hand, is controlled voluntarily. Skeletal muscles are connected to bones to power the body's movement. They consist of muscle fibers that stretch and relax in a way that is similar to a cluster of rubber bands. Skeletal muscles can be strengthened and made bigger—known as muscular hypertrophy—through exercise.

Developing larger, stronger skeletal muscles is an ongoing process that happens by gently overworking a specific muscle or muscle group until the fibers of muscle tissue become slightly damaged. The body quickly repairs the muscle tissue, making it a little hardier in the process to withstand further use. A few days after being overused, the muscle tissue will not only be healed, but it will also be slightly larger and stronger than before. Over time, as an athlete repeatedly breaks down skeletal muscle tissue and allows it to heal, muscles grow in mass and strength.

For soccer players, developing strong leg muscles is important for everything from kicking to maintaining balance during a game. "Players who get knocked off the ball or land on the ground need to improve their footwork and the strength of their hamstrings and quadriceps to enhance their balance," McEachen has said. "The true test is if a player can maintain a good base of support in all situations while competing."[19] Muscular legs not only bring better balance but also more powerful kicks. Large muscles are heavier than small muscles. Since

Soccer players often spend time in the gym, working on developing and strengthening their muscles.

FREE KICKS The human body has more than 600 muscles. Dozens of them are in the feet and legs.

the leg acts like a club during a kick, a heavier leg will swing harder and contact the ball with more force. Strong legs with a good amount of muscle mass are often an advantage for soccer players. During training, a soccer player may concentrate on adding bulk to the lower body using weightlifting techniques to develop the quadriceps on the front of the thigh and the hamstrings along the back of the thigh.

Being too muscular, however, can be a disadvantage in soccer. Precisely because muscle tissue is so heavy, soccer players should not have too much of it weighing down their legs. A soccer game requires a great deal of running. Running on legs that are twice as heavy as every other players' because of their muscle mass could affect another crucial aspect of a soccer player's physical fitness: endurance. This is the ability to remain physically active for long periods without tiring. It is important but needs to be balanced with other attributes.

PLAYING ON

Endurance is important when playing soccer. Teams whose players can tolerate intense physical activity from the beginning of a soccer match to the end improve their chances of winning. Teams whose players are exhausted and gasping for air by the end of a match may not fare as well. Just as athletes train their muscles to become bigger and stronger, they also train their entire body to improve their endurance. They may begin training by jogging long distances to prepare their body to run the equivalent of several miles every game. However, soccer is not played in a continuous sprint but in repeated bursts of running, broken up by periods of walking, jogging, jumping, and even moving backward. Soccer players must develop endurance, which is also known as stamina, for these demanding activities. One way they do this is by aerobic exercise, which is exercise that is powered by oxygen, such as running for at least 30 minutes.

Although aerobic exercise is important in soccer training, it is not the only kind of exercise required. This is because soccer does not call for the same level of energy to be used at all times. The ability of the muscles to produce bursts of speed even when the body becomes tired is important in soccer. Repeated sprints that raise a person's heart rate beyond the level of typical aerobic exercise are a form of anaerobic exercise—exercise that requires more than the oxygen normally needed by a working muscle, forcing the muscle to break down carbohydrates for energy. This process is called glycolysis, and it creates a byproduct called lactic acid, which builds up in the muscles and makes them feel sore and tired. Every time a muscle is used anaerobically, however, it becomes stronger and better adapted to the activity. Endurance training that demands many short sprints helps a soccer player build muscles that can handle the repeated anaerobic demands of a soccer game.

"The endurance of a soccer athlete is more than just being able to run forever," soccer coaches Sigi Schmid and Bob Alejo have said. "A high level of endurance will allow the soccer athlete to maintain nearly perfect execution of skills at close to 100 percent effort throughout a match."[20] This can be very hard to achieve. Players have to be careful to push in a way that is safe and effective for their body to build up this kind of endurance without harming themselves. For this reason, it is important to have the oversight of a coach or experienced trainer.

FUEL FOR THE BODY

Training is important. However, it can only do so much. Even the fittest athletes will be limited in their abilities if they do not eat properly and drink enough liquids, because the body depends on having the right types and amounts of nutrients and fluids to work efficiently. An athlete's body requires a constant store of carbohydrates, for example, because living cells convert them into glucose, which is a molecule that releases energy when it is broken apart. Carbohydrates that are not immediately used by cells are stored in the body as glycogen and later converted into glucose as the body's activity levels require. If soccer players do not eat enough

It is important for athletes to make sure they're eating enough.

carbohydrates to create glycogen reserves in the body before a match, they will run out of glucose before the end, and their starved, fatigued muscles will perform poorly. Even the brain needs glucose for energy to carry out essential soccer tasks such as decision making and maintaining coordination and reflexes, so a player who does not eat enough may have a poor mental performance on the field in addition to a poor physical performance.

Some people mistakenly believe athletes require protein more than any other nutrient, but carbohydrates that come from rice, pasta, whole grains, and vegetables are the mainstay of an athlete's diet. This is especially true of complex carbohydrates, which provide energy for long periods of time. Whole grains, beans, and vegetables are the best sources of complex carbohydrates.

Carbohydrates, not protein, are the primary form of energy used by all parts of the body—from the muscles to the brain. However, protein is still necessary for athletes. It is used in the body for building and repairing muscles. Fish, chicken, and eggs are common sources of protein for many athletes, including soccer players.

Soccer players also need to drink a lot of water to stay hydrated if they expect to reach their full potential during a practice or a game. They lose a lot of water through sweat during a match, and water is necessary in the body for many reasons. Having adequate water in the body helps lubricate the joints so they do not stiffen during a game. It also helps muscles contract quickly so that every time a soccer player wants to kick the ball, the muscles respond. Water is needed to bring oxygen to the muscles, and it flushes out some of the lactic acid produced when muscles work anaerobically. Water also helps keep the brain working even when the rest of the body is fatigued. A well-hydrated player feels less tired during a game, pays better attention, and is less likely to feel sore the following day.

The physical effects of dehydration, or lack of sufficient water in the body, can be devastating. Sports nutrition expert Don MacLaren stated, "A mild degree of dehydration will impair skilled performance and affect strength, stamina, and speed. An adequate fluid intake is necessary to offset the effects of dehydration."[21] Soccer players drink water throughout the day so they are well hydrated long before they begin to exercise and sweat heavily. It is also important for them to drink throughout a practice or a game. If an athlete's body lacks essential fuel and fluids, it will not matter how much or how well they train.

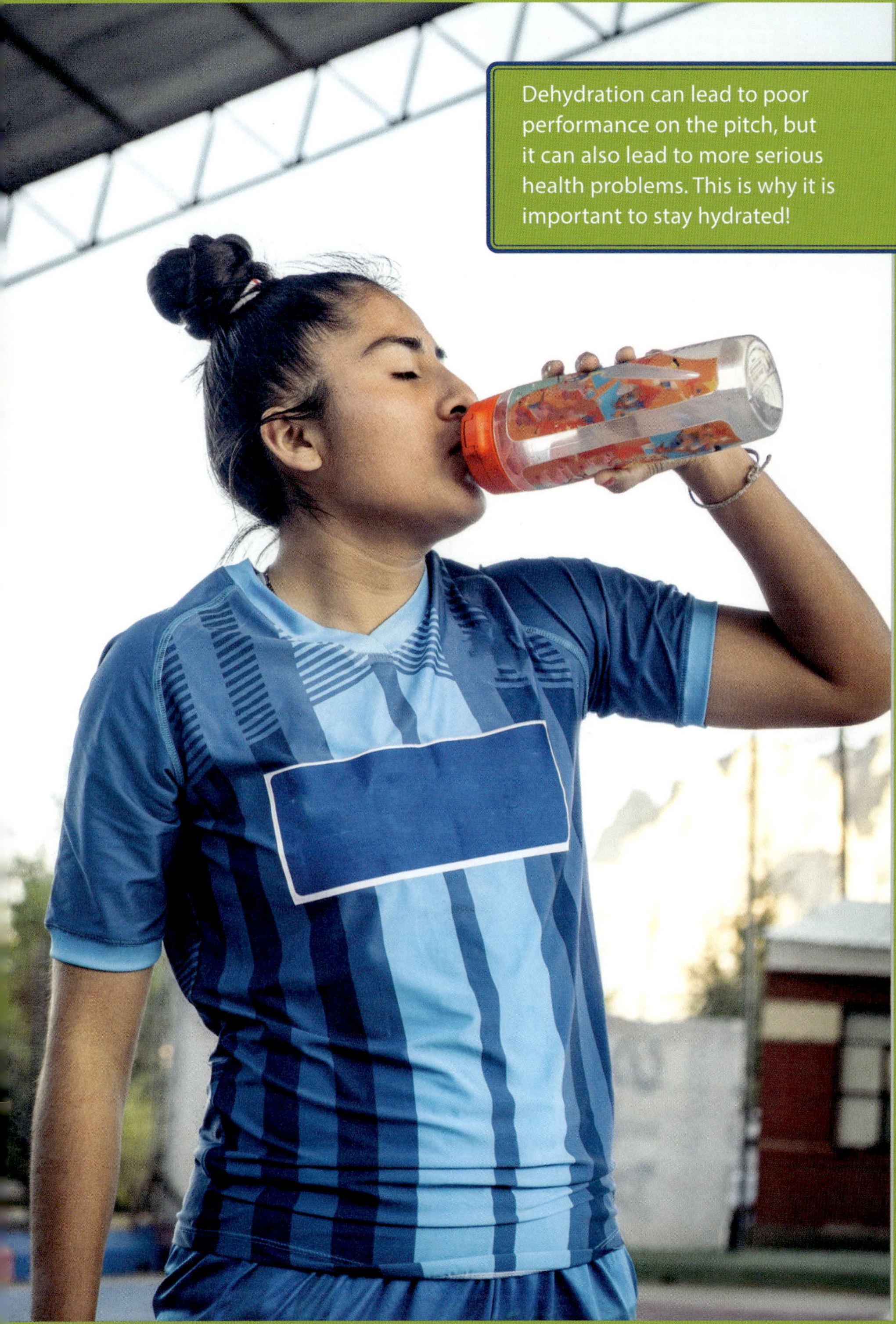

Dehydration can lead to poor performance on the pitch, but it can also lead to more serious health problems. This is why it is important to stay hydrated!

FREE KICKS Plyometrics was first used by athletes from the Soviet Union in the 1950s. Over the next few decades, this form of training spread throughout the world.

EXPLOSIVE EXERCISES

Many different conditioning exercises have been used by soccer players throughout the sport's history. As understanding of the human body and its development has improved, so has the effectiveness of training methods. In recent years, a type of training called plyometrics has become popular because of its success. Plyometrics involves explosive exercises that quickly stretch and contract muscles, exerting maximum force in short intervals of time. Stretching makes muscles longer, and contracting shortens them. Doing exercises that stretch and contract muscles increases muscle power and speed. Jumping is a common plyometric exercise, and soccer players use different kinds of jumps from different positions in their plyometric training.

STRETCH IT OUT

Soccer players who keep themselves well-fed and well-hydrated start out at an advantage. They will build muscle more efficiently and have more endurance than those who are dehydrated or undernourished. This also lowers the risk of getting sore or injured during a practice or a game. However, even the fittest and best-nourished soccer players may develop stiff muscles and be more likely to sustain an injury if they focus only on strength and endurance training and ignore flexibility, or the ability of muscle tissue to stretch for a greater range of motion. This is a key component of physical fitness and one that good soccer players spend time developing.

All skeletal muscles work by stretching and contracting, and like a rubber band, the more often they are stretched, the more pliable they become. Muscles that are not stretched regularly may remain constantly contracted. Since muscles create all their power by contracting, or flexing, to move a bone, a muscle that is already contracted cannot flex any more to help the leg swing into a

Stretching is essential for avoiding injuries, and it can also reduce soreness after an intense practice or match.

kick, for example. This can happen in muscles that are overdeveloped through too much exercise. People who have this problem are said to be "muscle bound," and this problem weakens a muscle, even if it is large and well developed from strength training.

Stretching exercises improve muscle flexibility, enhancing a muscle's ability to create motion. Many stretching exercises involve holding the body in a specific position to lengthen the muscles. Flexibility is one of the most important aspects of training for soccer players. Not only does it improve their playing, but it is also critical for preventing sports injuries. No matter how hard soccer players work on improving their coordination and reflexes or how physically fit they become, an injury can bring a player's career to an end. Athletes should learn about the causes of common injuries in their sport. This way, they have a better chance to train and compete in a way that helps them stay healthy. This can also help them play their best within those parameters.

CHAPTER FIVE

THE RISK OF INJURY

All sports can be a lot of fun, but there is always some risk of injury that cannot be fully avoided. Soccer especially can be a physically demanding sport. At a high level, it pushes an athlete's body to its limits and sometimes beyond. Injuries in soccer can come from overuse of body parts, contact with other players, improper conditioning, or accidents and seemingly random occurrences. For example, in 2020, Mexican soccer player Raúl Jiménez suffered a fractured skull after a collision with another player during a match. He could not play for nine months afterward and had no memory of the accident, or indeed the match itself. He returned to international soccer but now must wear a headguard for the rest of his career.

Soccer is a contact sport, which means players often hit each other or an object (in this case, the soccer ball) with some amount of force. Although there is a risk of injury due to contact, it is not as high as in many collision sports, such as American football, which are sports that feature athletes purposely hitting each other with great force.

Injury prevention and treatment is an important part of understanding soccer. Dislocated joints, broken bones, pulled or torn muscles, and concussions are just some of the most common injuries soccer players suffer on the pitch. It is important to know what causes these injuries, as well as what can be done to prevent them. Knowing what methods are used to treat them most effectively also can help players stay as safe as possible and keep their soccer career going.

Raúl Jiménez is shown here before he suffered his serious injury in 2020.

ANKLES AND FEET

The most common soccer injuries tend to be lower-body injuries, and there is one particular body part that is most at risk: the ankle. Soccer players perform many sprints and sudden turns and have frequent contact with the feet and legs of other players, all of which can put unnatural force on the ankles. The ankle joint consists of four bones: the tibia and the fibula, the long bones that form the shin; the talus, a small bone that creates a ball-and-socket joint by fitting into the socket where the bases of the fibula and tibia meet; and the calcaneus, or heel bone, which supports the talus. All four bones are held together by ligaments—tough, elastic-like bands that attach bones to each other at joints. There are four major ligaments in the ankle. Three are on the lateral side, facing away from the opposite ankle, and one is on the medial side (sometimes called the deltoid ligament), facing the opposite ankle. The ankle is a strong joint, designed to hold up throughout a lifetime of walking, running, and jumping, but it is not immune to severe damage, such as the major twisting that can happen during a soccer game.

If the ankle twists hard enough, the ligaments will stretch beyond their natural range of motion and may tear, either slightly or completely. Damage caused by the wrenching of ligaments is called a sprain, which is a serious injury that can take weeks or months to heal. Ankle sprains are some of the most common soccer injuries.

Sometimes, the wrenching or twisting motion is powerful enough to dislocate a joint, or pull the ball portion of one bone out of the socket portion of another. A dislocated joint often causes ligament damage and can cut off the blood supply to the affected area. Dislocations are serious injuries that require emergency medical treatment. They can happen with any joint, but because ankles are such sturdy joints, a dislocated ankle rarely happens unless a collision breaks a shinbone.

KNEE ISSUES AND INJURIES

Knees are another major joint that can be another common site of injury in soccer players. The knee is a hinge joint, or a joint that moves only back and forth. It connects the femur bone of the thigh to the tibia, the thicker of the shin's two parallel bones. The patella, a small bone often called the kneecap, is part of this joint as well. There is a pad of cartilage between the femur and the tibia called the meniscus, which acts as a cushion between the leg bones.

Several important ligaments connect the parts of the knee. The collateral ligaments run along the inner and outer sides of the joint and prevent the tibia from swinging side to side instead of front to back. Two cruciate ligaments, so named because they cross each other to form an X ("cruciate" means "cross shaped"), prevent the knee joint from rotating or twisting too much. One of these ligaments, the anterior cruciate ligament (ACL), keeps the knee from hyperextending, or moving beyond its natural range of motion. The other, the posterior cruciate ligament (PCL), keeps the tibia from moving too far backward.

Sprained or torn knee ligaments happen often in soccer. A tear to the ACL happens when the knee is forced to twist

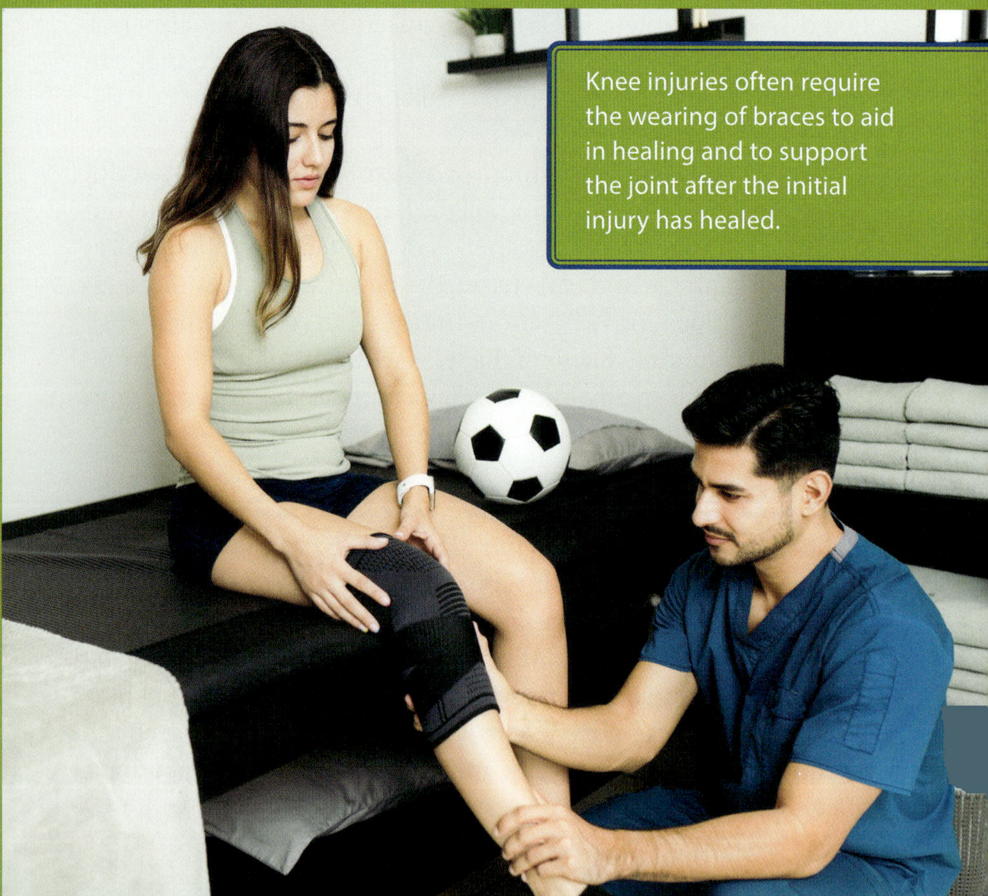

Knee injuries often require the wearing of braces to aid in healing and to support the joint after the initial injury has healed.

FREE KICKS Female soccer players have a higher risk of tearing their ACL than male soccer players.

unnaturally. This is a common and serious soccer injury. An ACL can be torn if a sprinting player suddenly stops running to change direction or if a player's lower leg is held down by another player during an attempted turn.

A torn knee ligament such as the ACL usually requires surgery and months of physical therapy—a kind of supervised exercise program that targets an injured body part to rebuild mobility and strength. Many soccer players return to the game once a torn ligament is healed, but previously damaged joints tend to be weaker, more painful, and prone to repeat injuries. "Because of the unusual stresses placed on knees in soccer," Richard Witzig has stated, "serious knee injuries are the most common physical injury to force retirement. Indeed, more than 30% of former players will experience chronic pain … on retirement."[22] Such injuries can haunt athletes long after they stop playing.

TEARS AND TENDONS

Through working out and careful training, athletes can make their muscles stronger. This is unlike ligaments, which cannot be strengthened to handle more stress. However, muscles can still be a site of serious injury for soccer players. They are especially vulnerable when a player's body is tired. Overexertion, or doing more physical activity than the body can handle, sometimes results in muscle damage. Colliding with another player can also harm muscles. Such situations can tear a muscle's fibrous tissue. In soccer, the most common site for muscle tears, sometimes referred to as pulled or strained muscles, are the hamstrings, which are groups of muscles that run along the back of the thighs.

There are three levels, or grades, of muscle tears. A grade 1 tear involves less than 5 percent of the muscle but causes pain and stiffness. Needing two to three weeks to heal, a grade 1

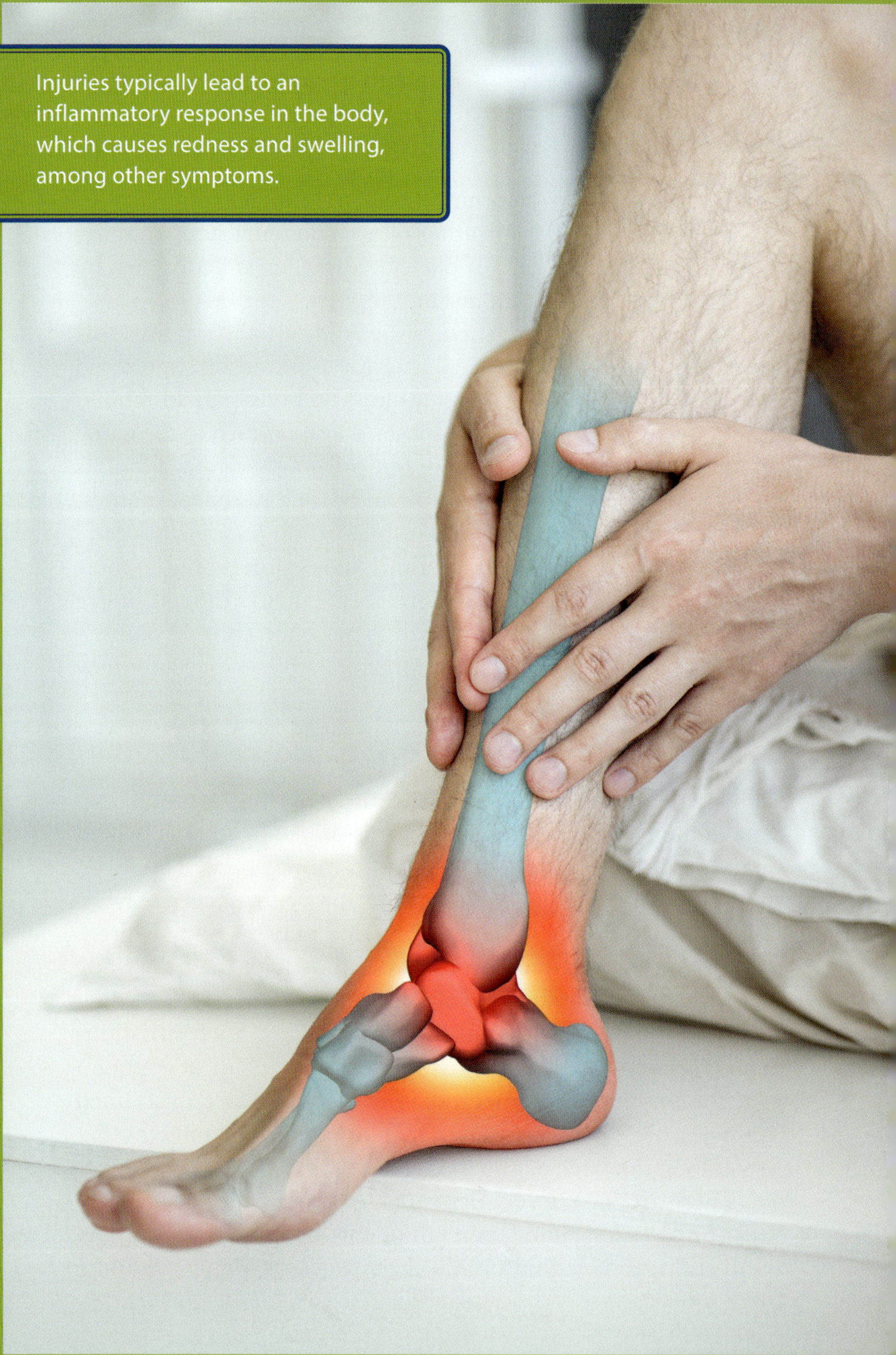

Injuries typically lead to an inflammatory response in the body, which causes redness and swelling, among other symptoms.

FREE KICKS The Achilles tendon is the biggest tendon in the human body. It is named after the Greek warrior.

muscle tear usually causes no additional problems, but if the player does not rest the muscle, the pain often does not get better. A grade 2 muscle tear involves breakage across much of the muscle's tissue but stops short of tearing the muscle completely in two. A player who suffers a second-degree tear usually cannot contract the muscle at all without severe pain. This kind of tear often involves swelling. A grade 3 muscle tear is a rupture, which is a complete tear that separates the muscle in two. The muscle is then completely unable to contract, and the player cannot move the affected limb normally. The torn ends of the ruptured muscle may ball up to form large lumps under the skin, and sometimes a gap can be felt under the skin where the muscle separated. This injury also causes internal bleeding at the site of the rupture. Ruptured muscles sometimes require surgery to join the pieces of muscle back together. Even after the muscle heals, scar tissue remains. This weakens and stiffens the muscle and makes it vulnerable to future injuries.

Just as muscles cannot work properly when badly torn, a muscle will be useless if its tendon, the band of fibrous tissue that connects it to a bone, is damaged. One of the most important tendons for soccer players is the Achilles tendon. The Achilles tendon is essential for walking, running, and jumping, but the force put on this tendon during an aggressive soccer game is sometimes too much. If the tendon tears, either partly or completely, then the calf muscle will be unable to contract normally. Without its anchor to the heel, the muscle may ball up in the back of the leg. The player will be unable to run or even walk. When David Beckham tore his Achilles tendon in 2010, his coach described what happened to his muscle: "He felt the muscle begin to come up, which is a typical symptom when you break an Achilles tendon."[23]

An injured Achilles tendon often requires surgery. It takes a long time to come back from this, and the rehabilitation process involves months of physical therapy to regain strength and range of motion. Sometimes, a comeback is not possible.

FRACTURED

Injuries to ligaments, muscles, and tendons can be dangerous and painful for athletes. This is also true of the bones to which these muscles, ligaments, and tendons attach, especially in the lower leg. They are also put into many risky situations during a game. High-speed, high-force kicks and tackles in soccer often pit one player's feet and shins against another's, causing a clash of bones. Bones are strong, but they can be damaged by a forceful blow, such as a high-speed collision between soccer players. A crack or break in a bone's surface is called a fracture.

Bones consist of a dense outer covering called compact bone, which surrounds a core of spongy bone (also known as cancellous bone), and bone marrow, where blood cells are produced. A fracture in a bone's surface is a serious injury that usually causes severe pain and swelling in the tissues surrounding the bone. Most bone fractures require medical treatment, which includes repositioning the broken bone and encasing the limb in a cast for several weeks to give the bone time to heal.

Some fractures are worse than others. The best-case scenario for a broken bone is a closed or simple fracture—a crack in the bone that does not cause part of the bone to shift and damage surrounding tissue and break the skin. A worse kind of break is a compound or open fracture, in which the bone on either side of the fracture spears into surrounding tissue or even pierces through the skin. Compound fractures can cause serious bleeding and tissue damage as well as excruciating pain. They require surgery and the use of plates, screws, and wires to realign the bones properly. A third type of fracture is a comminuted fracture, or a fracture in which the bone shatters into pieces. This kind of fracture may also require surgery and a long period of recovery during which the bone must be kept immobile in a cast in order to heal.

WORKING AS A PHYSICAL THERAPIST

Physical therapists are health-care professionals who develop individualized plans of treatment for patients who cannot move and function normally because of an injury or other medical condition. Physical therapists help athletes recover after a severe injury, such as a broken bone or a torn muscle, ligament, or tendon. They create a plan for each patient to reduce pain, restore range of motion, and keep muscles strong and flexible while the patient is recovering. Physical therapists help injured athletes return to competition as quickly as possible. They need a master's or doctorate degree in physical therapy and must pass their state's required examinations in order to obtain a license to practice. They are employed by hospitals, clinics, or private practices and often work evenings and weekends to fit their patients' schedules. In addition to a strong background in science, including physics, biology, and anatomy, they must have good interpersonal skills and empathy when working with athletes, who often need special encouragement and may fear their career in their sport is over after a severe injury.

Physical therapy is an important part of recovery for many injuries.

At the college level and in professional leagues, where soccer players move fast and are very physical and competitive, bone injuries are more common. Because severely broken bones are some of the most shocking and memorable injuries that occur on a soccer field, they receive a lot of attention from spectators, coaches, referees, and players. After a particularly bad incident, the player who caused a collision is sometimes accused of foul play. However, in a game as fast-paced as soccer, players know collisions hard enough to break bones are bound to happen.

Although serious injuries such as broken bones are not as common among youth soccer players, there has been a rise in such injuries among children in recent years. Experts believe increased physical play on the pitch is responsible for a rise in injuries. Brian Hafter, a coach and referee in girls' soccer leagues in California, stated, "There's no question that nowadays the players are much more physical, challenging for the ball, and as a result, can put themselves and their opponents in situations that can lead to more serious injuries."[24]

HEADING OFF CONCUSSIONS

Soccer players can also be at risk of head injuries, as Raúl Jiménez's 2020 injury and others show. Soccer is a unique sport in that players typically wear no helmet or other protective headgear, yet they frequently strike their head against the ball to stop its progress, move it up the field, or try to score a goal. Some sports medicine experts suspect that repeatedly heading the ball might cause many small head injuries that accumulate to cause brain damage in some players, which is similar to the way professional boxers sometimes suffer brain damage from taking repeated blows to the head and face. A study published in February 2017 revealed that repeatedly heading the ball—something soccer players do often in practice—increases a soccer player's risk of developing concussion symptoms.

A concussion is a serious brain injury that happens when the head is hit or jolted in a way that causes it to move back

Shown here is former U.S. Paralympic goalkeeper Sean Boyle, who wore a special kind of headgear to protect himself on the pitch.

HANDLING STRESS

The mental health of athletes is as important as their physical health. Elite athletes, such as those playing soccer in college or professionally, are often under a lot of stress and place a lot of pressure on themselves to succeed. Athletes who are trying to come back from an injury or who have experienced a period of poor play known as a slump deal with additional stressors. It is helpful for athletes to prioritize their mental health the same way they take care of their physical health, so it is not unusual for athletes to see sports psychologists to help them deal with the pressure of competing at a high level.

Sports psychologists are professionals who help athletes cope with the psychological and emotional stresses that can affect how they perform. A sports psychologist may work with an athlete to develop healthy attitudes toward games and matches, decrease their performance anxiety, increase their self-esteem, and help them cope with an injury or difficult loss on a big stage. Sports psychologists need at least a master's degree in psychology, paired with knowledge of sports science and experience working with athletes. Sports psychologists may work for a professional sports team; for a high school, college, or university; or in private practice.

and forth too rapidly. This causes the brain to move around in the skull in a dangerous way. Only 7 percent of soccer injuries suffered by children ages 7 to 17 are concussions, but they are among the most serious injuries that can occur during a match or practice. Severe concussions in soccer are more often a result of hitting another player, a goal post, or the ground than heading the ball. Sometimes, soccer players dive or fall to the ground, and their head is suddenly on the same level as other players' kicking feet. Goalkeepers often find themselves in such a position as they lunge for the ball to keep the other team from scoring. These incidents can result in an accidental kick to the head. Even more than a broken bone or a tear to a muscle, tendon, or ligament, a head injury can remove a player from the game of soccer permanently.

Soccer players wear shin guards to protect their legs, but they don't often wear protective gear for their head.

An extensive amount of research has been done in recent years on concussions and their long-term effects on a person's health. This has led to a sharp increase in awareness of the danger of brain injuries and the importance of evaluating athletes who have experienced a hit to the head for concussion symptoms, which include dizziness, blurry vision, and nausea. Although it may seem frightening to see that the rate of head injuries among youth soccer players increased by nearly 1,600 percent from 1990 to 2014, experts believe that dramatic increase is due in part to more people reporting and treating concussions in the correct way. Dr. Andrew Gregory, a professor at Vanderbilt University Medical Center, stated, "[The] concussion rate [is] going up … across the board … because [of] increased recognition … There are state laws [that say] if you have concussions you have to be seen. Parents, physicians, coaches, and players are more aware of it."[25] This increased awareness has led to increased safety measures, not just in soccer, but in all sports. Pro leagues for many sports have instituted more in-depth concussion protocols as well.

PLAY SAFE!

Soccer players do not wear much protective gear. A player's protection mainly comes from shin guards worn under their socks to minimize pain and injury to these sensitive spots caused by getting kicked or hit by the ball. Soccer players can also wear other protective gear if they want to, as long as it does not endanger other players or provide a distinct competitive advantage. Some soccer players choose to wear a mouth guard to protect their teeth and gums, and some wear special padded shorts to help protect their legs or headgear to protect their head.

As people learn more about what causes common soccer injuries, that knowledge is put to use to make it safer for those who play the sport. Technological advancements such as protective headgear and better concussion monitoring will make the future of the sport safer.

CHAPTER SIX

IN THE FUTURE

The modern game of soccer is not so different from the sport that first took off in the 1800s. You can still play it essentially with a ball, an open space, and two goals. Still, that doesn't mean that the sport has not evolved over the years. It has, and it continues to do so! New technology has been developed and incorporated to further goals such as making the game safer, making training more effective, and creating a better experience for fans.

Some of these technological advancements have included robot kickers, feet-powered fields, and smart balls. Inventors and engineers work to put the principles of science into practice when creating these new developments in how the sport of soccer is played.

BALL TECH

It likely seems that there's not much to change about the basic design of a soccer ball, and to some extent, this is true. However, more recent technology has been used to create better, more aerodynamic balls for events, including the World Cup. This technology helps to test and analyze the shape and tweak it.

Before the 2014 World Cup, the Brazuca soccer ball was put through many different tests to study its aerodynamics. Scientists in Japan tested the ball in a wind tunnel, which is a chamber in which air is blown at a known velocity past an object to study its aerodynamics. Wind tunnels are best known for testing aircraft, but they can also be used to test much smaller objects, such as soccer balls.

Scientists discovered that a smoother ball is actually a less ideal design than a ball that has small bumps or dimples on its surface. A smoother ball creates more drag, or air resistance, around it, which causes it to behave more unpredictably in the air. The ball used in the previous World Cup—the Jabulani—was relatively smooth, which made it difficult for goalkeepers to stop because of its unpredictable movement. Knowing this, the designers of the Brazuca created a ball that was covered with small bumps to decrease the drag around the ball.

The motion of the air around the Brazuca was difficult to see with the naked eye because air is invisible. However, scientists at the National Aeronautics and Space Administration (NASA) used lasers and smoke to show the movement of the air around a Brazuca ball in a wind tunnel in a way that could be easily seen. Scientists pumped smoke into the tunnel in a controlled fashion and used lasers to highlight the movement of the smoke at different speeds. The ball was also tested in a water channel that used dye that appears under a black light to show the movement of fluid around it.

The testing of the Brazuca was seen by employees at NASA as a fun way to get people interested in aerodynamics. As Rabi Mehta, chief of the Experimental Aero-Physics Branch at NASA's Ames Research Center in Moffett Field, California, said, "Sports provide a great opportunity to introduce the next generation of researchers to our field of aerodynamics by showing them something they can relate to."[26]

The Brazuca was tested in another creative way by Japanese scientists. They built a robot kicker to test soccer balls. The robot kicked each ball many times, with the scientists changing its positioning so different parts of its robotic foot connected with the ball. These tests were more reliable than human testing because the researchers could completely control the robot kicker, ensuring more accurate results.

GIVE IT THE BOOT

Soccer does not take much equipment to play, but besides the ball, the cleats, or boots, may be most important. So, it

The Adidas Conext 15 Final Vancouver used the same technology as the Brazuca. It was the first soccer ball created specifically for a Women's World Cup final.

THE ROBOT WORLD CUP

Robots are not used only to test soccer balls; they also play soccer on teams and in leagues. In 1997, the first official Robot World Cup—commonly known as RoboCup—conference and games were held. RoboCup is an initiative designed to promote interest in and awareness of robotics and artificial intelligence (AI) systems. It aims to do this by offering the public a relatable and entertaining platform to view robotic achievements, as scientists and engineers work toward a particular goal. That goal, as stated by RoboCup officials, is that "[b]y the middle of the 21st century, a team of fully autonomous humanoid robot soccer players shall win a soccer game, complying with the official rules of FIFA, against the winner of the most recent World Cup."[1] RoboCup developers believe such as goal is attainable because it only took 50 years for the invention of the airplane to develop into the space program and for the creation of the first digital computer to lead to the first computer to beat a human at chess.

Although no robot team is ready yet to take on their human counterparts in a soccer match, RoboCup events held between robot teams take place around the world every year. These events are attended by passionate fans of both soccer and robotics.

1. "Objective," RoboCup, 2016. www.robocup.org/objective.

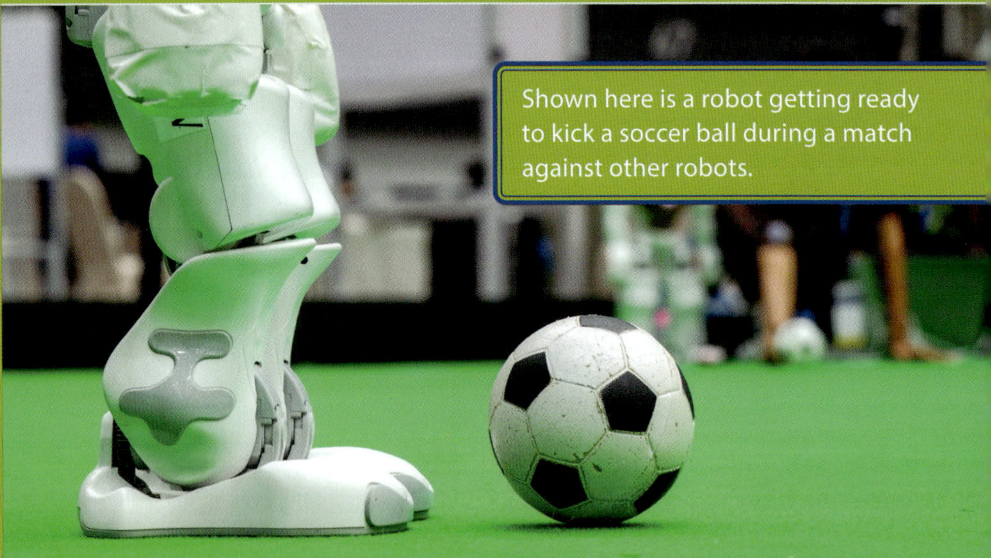

Shown here is a robot getting ready to kick a soccer ball during a match against other robots.

makes sense that these go through the same kind of serious testing that soccer balls have gone through. A number of companies do this, with one example being the U.S. company Nike. For years, the company has used newer technology to design and test their shoes, which, for soccer, now include the Phantom VNM and Phantom VSN as well as the Nike Mercurial Vapor cleats notably worn by soccer player Cristiano Ronaldo.

One earlier example of Nike's cleat design process is illustrated by the Magista 2 shoes. The Magista 2 was designed with the help of a system called Finite Element Analysis (FEA). This is a computer system that aims to accurately predict how a product, such as a soccer boot, will react in the real world. By using the FEA system, designers at Nike were able to figure out the best placement of studs on the bottom of the shoes to create the ideal amount of friction on any surface in any weather.

The different patterns of studs were quickly created using a 3D printer. This process was seen as a game-changer for athletic shoe development. Now, a new design could be printed in hours, where before the development of 3D printing technology, it would have taken weeks or months. As Nathan VanHook, a senior design director at Nike Football, said, "You see things right away … We can take the lever and say, 'Let's see what the most extreme [thing to do] is,' and are able to prototype and iterate superfast."[27]

The amount of research that went into the creation of the Magista 2 could even be seen in the color patterns on the shoe itself. Areas of the foot that are most likely to come into contact with the ball are highlighted with red. These areas were discovered through long periods of testing using motion capture technology. With more than 20 cameras and an advanced 3D system, Nike's lab captured the movements of athletes kicking and controlling a soccer ball. Designers then used the footage the cameras captured to model how the foot and ball interact in different situations. This technology has since become even more in-depth and futuristic.

FREE KICKS Other major brands that create soccer shoes are Adidas and Puma. The brands often have endorsement contracts with star players who wear their shoes. These deals can be for millions of dollars a year.

A TURF WAR

The 2015 Women's World Cup was played in Canada on artificial turf. This became a major news story because this event was the first FIFA World Cup—for men or women—to be played on a surface other than natural grass. Arguments were made in the lead-up to and in the aftermath of the tournament both for and against the use of artificial turf on the game's biggest stage.

Artificial turf is a synthetic, or man-made, surface designed to look, feel, and behave like real grass. Those in favor of its use believe it saves money because it does not require watering, fertilizing, or care such as cutting. Artificial turf also allows games to be played even in the rain, which would damage natural grass. Although there are many people who have supported the use of artificial turf, a large number of soccer players spoke out against its use. They have stated that it is difficult to predict how a ball will bounce on turf, and they have complained about the heat on the field, which has been known to melt players' cleats.

Before the 2015 World Cup, women's soccer players, such as U.S. star Sydney Leroux, voiced their concerns about playing on artificial turf. Leroux was especially concerned about the "turf burns" players sustain when they slide on artificial turf:

It's really sad women have to be guinea pigs for this. Once every four years it is a dream to play in the World Cup. And to have to think, OK, we have the potential for seven games at the World Cup. The first couple games, I have to be careful and take care of my body because you saw my leg [which was covered in turf burns]. How am I supposed to play after that with the same aggressiveness? I can't come out completely bandaged up. We will have to figure out a way that when sliding, we can continue to play without chewing up our body. The issue is: How are you supposed to play with the legs that I had? And I'm sure it would be even worse in a World Cup, where you're giving everything and more.[28]

The turf burns sustained by soccer players are concerning for reasons beyond the pain that comes with them. Many players, parents of young players, and coaches have worried about the cancer risk posed by playing on artificial turf. One prevailing theory about the link between artificial soccer turf and cancer is that the rubber pellets—often pieces of old tires—used as filler can get into turf-burn cuts and cause cancer. Studies have been conflicting, and the debate continues.

Today, different leagues and regions have different rules about artificial turf. Female soccer players have filed lawsuits claiming discrimination over being forced to play on the material. As of 2025, FIFA now requires all World Cup matches to be played on natural grass.

This brings further new technology into the mix. The 2026 FIFA World Cup will take place in cities through North America, in the United States, Canada, and Mexico. However, eight of the 16 chosen stadiums for matches have artificial turf. This means that turf will need to be replaced with natural grass in a painstaking process, complicated more by fixed or retractable roofs in some stadiums.

GOAL OR NO GOAL?

It is not always easy to tell if a soccer ball has fully crossed a goal line before the goaltender comes in to make a save. As such, goal-line technology is another big advancement in soccer technology. While many people were initially against this technology (for a variety of reasons, including cost), as of 2025, FIFA and some other organizations are using it as a staple.

The technology includes the use of cameras and electronic devices to determine whether a goal has been scored. More than a dozen cameras capture the movement of the ball to give an accurate picture of whether or not it has completely crossed the line.

Shown here is a goal-line camera used to help officials determine if a goal has been scored.

AL RIHLA AND AL HILM

The Adidas Al Rihla and Al Hilm soccer balls that were used in the 2022 World Cup featured a number of technological advances. ("Al Rihla" means "the journey" in Arabic, while "Al Hilm" means "the dream.") They used sustainable technology, which included environmentally friendly materials such as water-based glues and inks. They were also "smart" balls, with internal sensors connected by artificial intelligence that could provide immediate and detailed data to referees. This was meant to help make offsides calls more accurate and faster.

Two of the Al Rihla balls went to space on a SpaceX mission before they were used in the World Cup, taking soccer into space and further connecting the sport to science and technology.

FREE KICKS FIFA began using goal-line technology in tournaments in 2012.

Decisions are not made by the tech alone. Referees consult the information to make a decision. This information is available very quickly (usually taking one second or less) and is sent directly to an official's device. It can also be used to create a 3D animation of the play for people watching in the stadium or on television.

Some systems also use a sensor in the soccer ball and at the goal lines to determine if the ball has crossed the line. There is still much criticism of the systems, which some dislike because it removes part of human element from the game and others reject because of the high costs.

Data and statistics are very important in the world of soccer. Technology can help players, coaches, trainers, and fans keep track of and compare useful numbers.

LIGHT IT UP

Soccer players generate a lot of kinetic energy as they run up and down the pitch every game. Some inventors have created a newer way to put soccer fields and all that kinetic energy to good use.

In 2014, a soccer field was opened in Brazil that used the kinetic energy from players' feet to power the lights around the field. A similar field opened in Nigeria in 2016.

These fields use tiles to collect the kinetic energy from the movement of players' feet, turning it into electricity that is stored until it is needed to power the floodlights that illuminate the fields after dark. Both fields also use solar panels to collect additional energy from the sun, which is used with the kinetic energy from the players to provide enough power to turn on the lights.

This creative use of renewable energy sources is important for developing countries, where electricity is still not available to everyone. The lighted fields are meant to be a safe place for people to play the sport they love after dark.

HEALTH MONITORING, BALL TRACKING

These days, training for soccer is also often technologically influenced. Wearable heart rate monitors have become common sights on many people—not just athletes—in recent years. Although that technology is still an important part of training for professional and college soccer players, it has been combined with other technological developments to produce even more personalized training programs.

As Dawn Scott, the strength and fitness coach for the U.S. Women's National Team (USWNT) explained:

> *Heart rate monitoring has been around for over 10 years now, but in the past five years there has been an increase in the use of GPS technology in soccer and sports generally, which is basically like a car's satellite navigation tracking every single movement and impact a player makes on the field.*[29]

Brazil, shown here, is so passionate about soccer that it even uses the sport to power some of its neighborhoods!

Wearable monitors record a player's heart rate and GPS and transmit that information back to trainers and coaches. This data is then used to determine the best training regimen and workload for each player. The GPS technology measures how much ground a player covers while running during practice, while the heart rate monitor measures how hard their body is working as they cover that ground. These two measurements are used together to indicate a player's overall level of fitness and to help coaches and trainers get them into game shape. As Scott said:

> *By combining the heart rate and GPS, firstly it allows you to determine how players cope with a certain workload and gives a good indication of the fitness level for players. If two players have the same external load from the GPS, but one player's heart rate is higher, it suggests that their endurance system is not as well developed ... Once you know the positional load you can then use that as a gauge and indication of your physical load during training, as well as ensure players are prepared for the load they will experience during a game.*[30]

Analyzing the GPS and heart rate data from the wearable monitors allows trainers and coaches to work with players to get them in their best shape without pushing them too hard. It ensures that players receive a manageable amount of playing time during a game, which can lead to more success on the pitch. More importantly, it helps them keep from over-exertion and injury.

Other newer forms of technology are also likely to spread to soccer pitches and stadiums around the world. One likely aspect is artificial intelligence, or AI, which could be used to power apps for stadium navigation and fan experience. Teams are also using it to analyze player and opponent performances. Only time will tell how this technology will be used in the future of soccer.

NOTES

Chapter One: The Most Popular Sport

1. Quoted in David Goldblatt, *The Ball Is Round: A Global History of Soccer*. New York, NY: Riverhead Books, 2006, p. 3.
2. Nigel B. Crowther, *Sport in Ancient Times*. Westport, CT: Praeger, 2007, p. 4.
3. Goldblatt, *The Ball Is Round*, p. 12.
4. Richard Witzig. *The Global Art of Soccer*. New Orleans, LA: Cusiboy Publishing, 2006, p. 9.
5. Quoted in Jean Fievet, "Will World Cup 2010 Be Most-Watched TV Event?," ABC News, June 11, 2010. abcnews.go.com/International/Media/world-cup-mania-kicks-off-world/story?id=10884963.
6. Witzig, *The Global Art of Soccer*, p. 7.

Chapter Two: Physics Lessons

7. John Wesson, *The Science of Soccer*. New York, NY: CRC Press, 2002, p. 72.
8. Seyed Hamid Hamraz and Seyed Shams Feyzabadi, "General Purpose Learning Machine Using K-Nearest Neighbors Algorithm." In *Robot Soccer World Cup IX*, edited by Ansgar Bredenfeld, Adam Jacoff, Itsuki Noda, and Yasutake Takahashi. Berlin, Germany: Springer-Verlag, 2006, p. 532.
9. Wesson, *The Science of Soccer*, p. 81.
10. Jim Puhalla, Jeff Krans, and Mike Goatley, *Sports Fields: A Manual for Design Construction and Maintenance*. Hoboken, NJ: John Wiley & Sons, 1999, p. 278.

Chapter Three: Science in Motion

11. Nate Scott, "Carli Lloyd Put on the Greatest World Cup Final Performance Ever," *USA Today*, July 6, 2015. ftw.usatoday.com/2015/07/carli-lloyd-put-on-the-greatest-world-cup-final-performance-ever.
12. Cameron Bauer, *Algebra for Athletes*, 2nd ed. New York, NY: Nova Science Publishers Inc., 2007, p. 96.
13. Gene Klein, "Corner Kicks and Throw-Ins." In *Attacking Soccer: Tactics and Drills for High-Scoring Offense*, edited by Joseph A. Luxbacher. Champaign, IL: Human Kinetics, 1999, p. 107.
14. Klein, "Corner Kicks and Throw-Ins," p. 107.
15. Peter Mellor and Tony Waiters, "Goalkeeping Excellence." In *The Soccer Coaching Bible*, edited by the National Soccer Coaches Association of America. Champaign, IL: Human Kinetics Publishers, Inc., 2004, p. 164.

Chapter Four: Training Smart

16. Witzig, *The Global Art of Soccer*, p. 25.
17. Ron McEachen, "Training for High-Level Soccer Fitness." In *The Soccer Coaching Bible*, edited by the National Soccer Coaches Association of America. Champaign, IL: Human Kinetics Publishers, Inc., 2004, p. 116.
18. Quoted in Gavin Mortimer, *A History of Football in 100 Objects*. London, UK: Serpent's Tail, 2012.
19. McEachen,"Training for High-Level Soccer Fitness," p. 118.
20. Sigi Schmid and Bob Alejo, *Complete Conditioning for Soccer*. Champaign, IL: Human Kinetics Publishers, Inc., 2002, p. 3.
21. Don MacLaren, "Nutrition." *In Science and Soccer*, 2nd ed., edited by Thomas Reilly and A. Mark Williams. New York, NY: Routledge, 2005, p. 73.

Chapter Five: The Risk of Injury

22. Witzig, *The Global Art of Soccer*, p. 108.
23. Quoted in Andrew Das, "Beckham's Achilles' Tendon 'Totally Torn,' According to Surgeon," Goal: The *New York Times* Soccer Blog, March 14, 2010. goal.blogs.nytimes.com/2010/03/14/injured-beckham-may-miss-world-cup/.

24. Quoted in Rachel Rabkin Peachman, "Broken Bones and Bruises Rise and Youth Soccer Gets Aggressive," *New York Times*, September 13, 2016. www.nytimes.com/2016/09/13/well/family/broken-bones-and-bruises-rise-as-youth-soccer-gets-aggressive.html.
25. Quoted in Shailja Metha, "Reported Concussions in Youth Soccer Soar 1,600 Percent in 25 Years, According to Study," ABC News, September 12, 2016. abcnews.go.com/Health/reported-concussions-youth-soccer-soar-1600-percent-25/story?id=42030150.

Chapter Six: In the Future

26. Quoted in Jonas Dino and Jerry Colen, "NASA Turns World Cup into Lesson in Aerodynamics," NASA, July 30, 2015. www.nasa.gov/content/nasa-turns-world-cup-into-lesson-in-aerodynamics.
27. Quoted in Edgar Alvarez, "Nike's Latest Soccer Cleat Is Its Most Data-Driven Shoe Yet," Endgadget, July 25, 2016. www.engadget.com/2016/07/25/nike-magista-2-nsrl-inside-look/.
28. Quoted in Julie Foudy, "Sydney Leroux: Why Turf Is Terrible for Soccer Players," ESNPW.com, November 13, 2014. www.espn.com/espnw/news-commentary/article/11868149/sydney-leroux-explains-why-turf-terrible-soccer-players.
29. Quoted in Megan Logan, "The Wearable Prepping the US Women's Soccer Team for Battle," *Wired*, June 22, 2015. www.wired.com/2015/06/wearable-prepping-us-womens-soccer-team-battle/.
30. Quoted in Logan, "The Wearable Prepping the US Women's Soccer Team for Battle."

GLOSSARY

anatomy: A branch of science that has to do with the structure of living things, especially the human body.

artificial intelligence (AI): A branch of computer science that deals with the simulation of intelligent behavior in computers.

central nervous system: The parts of the brain and spinal cord that receive and process stimuli from the body and coordinate appropriate physical responses.

dimensions: Mathematical measurements of the boundaries of an object or area.

endurance: The ability to tolerate difficult physical activity for a long period of time.

fatigue: The state of being very tired.

intravenous: Entering through a vein.

iterate: To say or do something more than once.

mass: The measurement of an object's size and how much material it contains.

molecule: The smallest particle of a substance that retains all the properties of that substance.

motion capture: Technology that digitally records specific movements and translates them into computer-animated images.

perimeter: The outer boundary of a geometric figure.

scar tissue: Connective tissue that forms a scar after injury.

stimulus: An event or condition in the environment that directly influences bodily activity in a living thing.

trajectory: The path of a moving object.

vestibular system: A system in the inner ear that is made up of three canals: the saccule, the utricle, and the semicircular canals.

FOR MORE INFORMATION

BOOKS

Berglund, Bruce. *Soccer GOATS: The Greatest Athletes of All Time*. North Mankato, MN: Capstone Press, 2024.

Clarke, David J. *Soccer Strategies*. Minneapolis, MN: SportsZone, 2024.

Harris, Beatrice. *STEM in Soccer.* Buffalo, NY: Cavendish Square Publishing, 2025.

Martin, Emmett. *Positions in Soccer*. Buffalo, NY: PowerKids Press, 2023.

Monning, Alex. *Soccer*. Minneapolis, MN: A & D Xtreme, 2023.

Schwartz, Heather E. *US Women's National Soccer Team: Winning On and Off the Field.* Minneapolis, MN: Lerner Publications, 2024.

WEBSITES

FIFA
www.fifa.com
FIFA's official website features articles, scores, photos, and videos for both men's and women's matches.

"NASA Turns World Cup into Lesson in Aerodynamics"
www.nasa.gov/content/nasa-turns-world-cup-into-lesson-in-aerodynamics
This article gives a detailed description of the tests NASA ran on the Brazuca soccer ball and has a video of those tests being conducted by NASA engineers.

"The Power of Innovation—Creating Energy with Footsteps"
www.youtube.com/watch?v=EpYRH-njaAI
This YouTube video focuses on the development of and the reaction to the technology that has allowed the lights around soccer fields in developing nations to be powered by footsteps.

RoboCup
www.robocup.org
The official RoboCup website presents a detailed history of RoboCup, a complete list of leagues and events, and galleries featuring photos and videos of robotic soccer players in action.

Safety Tips: Soccer
kidshealth.org/en/teens/safety-soccer.html
This website provides important information on how to stay safe and avoid injuries while playing soccer.

U.S. Soccer
www.ussoccer.com
Soccer fans and aspiring superstars can read articles about, view schedules for, and see match results for the U.S. men's and women's national teams.

U.S. Youth Soccer
www.usyouthsoccer.org
Coaches and players in the U.S. Youth Soccer program can find valuable information on this website, including videos, guides, and online education courses on topics that range from concussions to nutrition.

INDEX

T

U

V

W

PICTURE CREDITS

Cover, bokan/Shutterstock.com; Cover, pp. 1, 3-104 hero mujahid/Shutterstock.com; Cover, pp. 1, 3, 4, 6, 18, 34, 48, 63, 77, 87, 94, 96, 98, 103, 104 marooshka/Shutterstock.com; Cover, pp. 1, 3-104 Free Icon Download/Shutterstock.com; p. 5 matimix/Shutterstock.com; p. 8 Stray Toki/Shutterstock.com; p. 10 CK-TravelPhotos/Shutterstock.com; p, 11 https://commons.wikimedia.org/wiki/File:Giovanni-Stradano-Gioco-del-calcio-in-piazza-Santa-Maria-Novella-1561-62-1024x721.jpg; p. 12 ph.FAB/Shutterstock.com; p. 16 A.RICARDO/Shutterstock.com; p. 19 Shopidea Studio/Shutterstock.com; p. 21 Master1305/Shutterstock.com; p. 23 Andrey Burmakin/Shutterstock.com; p. 25 Alexander Gordeyev/Shutterstock.com; p. 26 WBMUL/Shutterstock.com; p. 29 Artem Grebenyuk/Shutterstock.com; p. 32 fifg/Shutterstock.com; p. 35 lev radin/Shutterstock.com; p. 37 Life science/Shutterstock.com; p. 40 koonsiri boonnak/Shutterstock.com; p 42 Julian Bohorquez/Shutterstock.com; p. 44 Fabrizio Andrea Bertani/Shutterstock.com; p. 46 Ground Picture/Shutterstock.com; p. 50 Drazen Zigic/Shutterstock.com; p. 54 Prostock-studio/Shutterstock.com; p. 57 Drazen Zigic/Shutterstock.com; p. 59 Jhon Percy Ticona Mamani/Shutterstock.com; p. 61 Stephen Coburn/Shutterstock.com; p. 64 sbonsi/Shutterstock.com; p. 66 antoniodiaz/Shutterstock.com; p. 68 staras/Shutterstock.com; p. 71 Gorodenkoff/Shutterstock.com; p. 73 IOIO IMAGES/Shutterstock.com; p. 75 sirtravelalot/Shutterstock.com; p. 79 urbanbuzz/Shutterstock.com; p. 80 FeelGoodLuck/Shutterstock.com; p. 84 Giorgio Rossi/Shutterstock.com; p. 86 alphaspirit.it/Shutterstock.com; pp. 88-89 Vadim_N/Shutterstock.com.

ABOUT THE AUTHOR

AMY B. ROGERS is an experienced nonfiction author who has written many books for young readers on topics that include American history, science, and women's participation in sports. She lives in a suburb of Buffalo, New York, with her husband, Steve, and their Welsh corgi, Jiminy.